THE
REPUBLICAN
PLAYBOOK

COPY 4478

PROPERTY OF

George W Bush

Place your right hand over this book and repeat the following:

By reading this book, I promise to swear in a court of law
that I have never read this book, I have never seen this book,
and that this book does not exist,
so help me GOP.

THE REPUBLICAN NATIONAL COMMITTEE

2006

CONTENTS

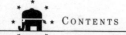

FROM: The Republican National Committee

TO: Valued Members of the Republican Elite

QUESTION: What is the one book that every Republican candidate, office holder, or supersecret covert operative has to read to kick some serious Democrat ass?

If you answered, "George W. Bush is living proof that Republicans don't have to read anything," you're right, up to a point, but that's not the answer we're looking for. Try again.

If you answered, *My Pet Goat,* you're correct that President Bush did read that book, but it's hard to make the argument that other Republicans should read it, or that reading it would in any way help us kick some serious Democrat ass. Actually, being seen reading *My Pet Goat* is something Republicans should avoid doing at all costs, especially if they see that tub o' lard Michael Moore sneaking up on them with his Communist, Saturn-driving camera crew. In fact, if you are reading *My Pet Goat* and you see Michael Moore and his nineteen chins sneaking up on you, hurl the book into the nearest bushes, look as nonchalant as possible, and then run like the wind. Although to be honest, if someone the size of a parade float is capable of sneaking up on you, you need to get your eyes checked, and pronto, my friend. Actually, the more we think about it, *My Pet Goat* was kind of a smartass answer on your part. Try again, and this time, be serious.

Note to self: Finish reading "My Pet Goat"

The Bible, you say? Well, that's a better answer, since there are parts of the Bible that are helpful to Republicans, like the part where God smites the people who try to give gay married couples medical benefits, and the part where Jesus turns the loaves and fishes into dividend tax cuts. But other parts of the Bible—like the turn-the-other-cheek part or the meek-inheriting-the-earth part or the Old Testament—not so much.

Give up?

The one book every Republican has to read is the book you are currently holding in your hands, sleeping with under your pillow, or clutching tightly between your legs: *The Republican Playbook.* And if you don't believe us, try this fact on for size: Not only has President Bush read *The Republican Playbook,* he carries it with him everywhere he goes—even when he goes to Crawford for his three-month summer vacation.

Unbelievable, you say? Read on.

On September 30, 2004, President Bush squared off in the first presidential debate against the Democrat presidential nominee, former hippie and Vietnam War traitor Sen. John Kerry (D-Mass.). Photos taken of the president, and later widely circulated on the Internet, showed that the president had what appeared to be a small rectangular bulge protruding from his suit jacket in the region between his manly, powerful shoulder blades. Members of the liberal-dominated media and homosexual blogocracy speculated that the bulge was created by a hidden radio receiver intended to feed the president clever responses during the debate, much like the device that Bill O'Reilly uses on his television program to help him stick to his script and avoid saying sexy things about loofahs. Others theorized that the bulge was a device that enabled Vice President Cheney to operate the president by remote control from the Vice President's subterranean lair buried miles beneath the Arctic Circle. And while it is true that Vice President Cheney has used a device exactly like that on occasion, specifically during every State of the Union address and presidential press conference, that was not the object bulging from between the President's shoulder blades on that memorable, victorious night.

It was *The Republican Playbook.*

That's right. President Bush knew what any Republican worth his Halliburton stock options has known for decades: that *The Republican Playbook* is the most lethal arrow in any Republican's quiver, something no Republican should ever leave home without, much like Batman's utility belt or Kate Moss's coke spoon. The president knew that if so-called Sen. Kerry landed

Return
XXX:
State
of the
Union
to
Block
buster

President George W. Bush hid The Republican Playbook *on his person during a 2004 debate with Sen. John Kerry (D-Mass.). Consulting the book while the TV cameras were not looking, he romped to an easy victory.*

any serious body blows on him during that all-important debate, he would be just fine, thank you very much, because he had *The Republican Playbook* secreted on his person. And next to having a shipload of Swift boat vets hiding in the shoulder-blade region of his suit jacket, *The Republican Playbook* was the best thing he could possibly have brought with him as he faced off against that flip-flopping, ketchup-marrying Democrat weasel from the Socialist Republic of Taxachusetts.

If, for example, Sen. Kerry touched him up on the issue of Iraq, he could have consulted the section entitled "Change the Subject Before the Subject Changes You," and accused Sen. Kerry of loving death-row escapees or trees. If Sen. Kerry charged him with squandering the federal budget surplus, he could have dipped into the section called "Use Movie Catchphrases to Make Your Point" and said, "Life is like a box of chocolates," stopping the Democrat in his tracks like a startled deer. And finally, in the worst-case scenario, if President Bush somehow lost the debate and found himself trailing in the polls by election day, he could have dipped into the chapter entitled "New Voting Booth Designs for Heavily Democrat Districts" and coasted to an easy second term.

Welcome, fellow Republican, to *The Republican Playbook*. And welcome to victory, the sweetest nectar a Republican will ever taste.

NOTE: If this copy of *The Republican Playbook* appears on eBay and can be traced back to you, you will be shot on sight.

In 1972, President Richard Nixon commissioned the very first edition of The Republican Playbook, *which contained a detailed blueprint for "Operation: Foolproof Plan," later known as the Watergate burglary.*

Keeping The Republican Playbook *in his left rear pants pocket early in his presidency often caused President Gerald Ford to lose his balance and fall down. He later carried an additional copy in his right pocket in order to maintain equilibrium, but by then his public image as a blithering idiot was already firmly in place.*

A chapter entitled "Deny Knowing Anything About Anything Going On at the White House" was particularly helpful to President Ronald Reagan during the so-called Iran-Contra scandal.

Although he carried it with him everywhere he went, the first President Bush ultimately did not need The Republican Playbook to win the 1988 election because the Democrats nominated Gov. Michael Dukakis (D-Mass.).

*After winning the election in 2003, California Gov.
Arnold Schwarzenegger credited* The Republican Playbook *with helping
him emphasize his modest accomplishments and deemphasize his
extensive record of groping women and praising Hitler.*

THE REPUBLICAN PLAYBOOK—FAQS

**HOW OFTEN IS *THE REPUBLICAN PLAYBOOK*
UPDATED?**

T*he Republican Playbook* is updated every two years, for each presidential and midterm election. Interestingly, though, the tactics contained in the original 1972 edition are little changed from those in the book you are currently reading, because the Democrats are just as easy to beat now as they were then. Most of the changes in the *Playbook* reflect advances in technology, like the advent of cell phones and the Internet, which enable us to spread lies and distortions at a much faster speed than ever before.

WHY IS *THE REPUBLICAN PLAYBOOK* SO SMALL?

T he book was designed to be portable, so that a Republican political candidate could carry it with him at all times in an inconspicuous manner. Also, it was important that it be tiny enough to elude detection in a full body-cavity search if the owner of the book winds up in prison. Case in point: Over 9,000 Republican politicians have been convicted since 1972, and none of them has had to part with the book while behind bars.

**CAN *THE REPUBLICAN PLAYBOOK*
BE USED AS A WEAPON?**

Y es, *The Republican Playbook* can and should be used as a weapon. The cover and spine of the book are fabricated from a superhard material, making the book a blunt object which can cause severe trauma to the skull of a Democrat. Also, the edges of the book's pages have been honed to a razor-like sharpness, capable of inflicting acute and potentially fatal paper cuts.

WHAT SHOULD I DO WITH
THE REPUBLICAN PLAYBOOK
IF I AM CAPTURED BY DEMOCRATS?

If you are captured by Democrats, you have three options. First, you can hide *The Republican Playbook* in one of your body cavities and, as long as you don't walk funny, they will never know it is there. Second, you can use *The Republican Playbook* as a weapon and kill the Democrats. Third, and this is very important to know, *The Republican Playbook* is made out of 100 percent edible material, so you can eat the book in its entirety. Starting in 2000, *The Republican Playbook* was made out of a new high-protein substance that will be consistent with your low-carb lifestyle, if you have one.

WILL *THE REPUBLICAN PLAYBOOK*
MAKE MY ASS LOOK BIG?

If carried in a rear pants pocket, yes, *The Republican Playbook* will make your ass look big. But in our view, having a big-looking ass is a small price to pay for victory in November.

†ALKING POINTS

The Democrat Party and Why It Is Bad

Despite the success of such wholly owned Republican Party subsidiaries as the FOX News Channel, Rev. Pat Robertson's *The 700 Club*, and Mel Gibson, a surprising number of Americans still do not know that the Democrat Party is bad, and why. Case in point: a recent survey conducted by the Gallup Organization shows that a majority of Americans persist in believing that the two-party system is "a good idea." Sure it is, right up there with flammable sleepwear and the avian flu. The following easy-to-digest facts-at-your-fingertips about the Democrats should help consign the idea of the two-party system to the place it belongs: the dustbin of history.

- The word "Democrat" comes from the Greek words "demos," meaning "demonic," and "cratos," meaning "creature." So even the ancient Greeks knew what is obvious to us today: that the Democrats are demonic creatures bent on destroying America.

- Democrats want to defend America with spitballs. In his keynote address to the Republican National Convention in 2004, former Democrat senator Zell Miller said of Democrat presidential nominee John Kerry, "This is the man who wants to be the Commander in Chief of our U.S. armed forces? U.S. forces armed with what? Spitballs?" No prominent Democrat has come forward to disavow the plan to defend America with spitballs, so it must be true.

- Every war in the history of the United States has been a "Democrat War," i.e., started by a Democrat. This is true of the Vietnam War, the Korean War, and most recently, the war in Iraq, which was started by lifelong Democrat Saddam Hussein.

- The Democrat Party traces its heritage back to 1792. However, had it existed before then, the following people would have been Democrats: Benedict Arnold, Genghis Khan, and Judas Iscariot.

- If the Democrats get their way, the only people in this country who would be allowed to own guns would be gay cowboys.

- If you jump into a swimming pool less than thirty minutes after having lunch with a Democrat, you will get cramps and drown.

Ask NSA — How much # to wiretap every Democrat in country?

TAP INTO THE MAGICAL POWER OF LYING

From time immemorial, lying has always been the Republican Party's most potent and reliable weapon. Given how useful and effective lying can be, it's amazing what a bad rap it gets. Why has lying fallen into such low repute? One theory: The liberal-dominated media wants to give lying a bad name, because even though Democrats try to lie, they're not as good at it as we are. The fact is, lying has always been an important part of a robust democracy, and we'll go one step further than that: Lying saves lives.

Example: the proverbial shouting "fire" in a crowded theater. Let's say you saw some flames and smoke in a theater, and decided because of the liberal bias against falsehood that it was a good time to tell the truth. By shouting "fire," you would create a stampede that might injure or even kill hundreds of people, unless the theater was showing a Ben Affleck film. However, if you chose to lie, and merely slipped out of the theater nonchalantly without telling anyone about the fire, no one would be hurt. So much for the damage lying supposedly does.

Many Republicans are under the impression that being a Republican makes you a born liar. Nothing could be further from the truth. Lying is an art, like singing or money laundering, and there's only one way to get good at it: practice, practice, practice. To develop your lying "chops," try these simple exercises.

- When you go to a party full of people you've never met, introduce yourself with a false name. If your name is "Dave," for example, say it's "Jim." As basic as this seems, it's an important exercise to get your lying muscle working. Before you know it, you'll be lying about the reason you invaded a country.

- When you are filling out your income tax return, do not list any household employees, even if you have three illegal Dominicans who have worked for you for the past twenty years and if one of them is CEO of five of your dummy corporations.

- When updating your resume before the next election, claim that you served five years as a Green Beret and won the Congressional Medal of Honor. If you are ever challenged to produce some members of your "band of brothers," mist up and say, "I was the only one who made it out of there alive."

FUNDRAISING LETTER FROM GOD

Invoking God's name has always been an effective fundraising tool for Republicans in years gone by, second only to lying about the opponent's war record. In recent years, however, Democrats have cried foul about the use of the Almighty in mass mailings, claiming that it violates the separation of church and state. Even though our party's position is that the separation of these two institutions is an outdated concept, and that significant economies of scale could be achieved if they were merged into one entity called "sturch," using God's name in fundraising letters isn't worth the grief we get for doing it. Instead, please use the following fundraising letter from God himself, which a group of prominent theologians led by the Rev. Jerry Falwell assures us is what God would write if he had access to a computer:

From the Desk of God

Dear _____,

As King of the Universe, I don't usually get involved in the rough-and-tumble of a political campaign, but this year is different, because there is so much at stake. That's why I'm writing to you to ask you to support_____, the Republican candidate for _____.

Now, you're probably saying to yourself, "I don't mean to take your name in vain, but God, are you kidding? Why do you need my help? You're omnipotent and omnipresent. If you want _____ to win, couldn't you just smite his foe, Democrat _____?"

Well, I'm glad you asked me that. The fact of the matter is, if I wanted to smite every Democrat in the country I could pick up a lightning bolt and do it. (Don't think I haven't been tempted—especially that jerk Howard Dean.) But the simple truth is, federal election law prohibits me from doing so.

But here's the good news: There is a way to smite the Democrats right here on Earth, and that's called negative campaign ads. And that's why it's so important that you send your money today.

One final thing: A lot of you have been asking me lately when the world is coming to an end. Well, I don't have an answer to that, but I'll tell you this much: When it comes time to end the world, I can think of no one who'd be better at helping me do it than Republican _____.

Yours in Heaven,

G

God

SCARE TACTIC:
THE SUPREME COURT

One of the Democrats' favorite ways to energize their base is by telling them the following: "If the Republicans are in power," they say, "they will pack the Supreme Court with right-wing whack-jobs who will have a stranglehold on the nation's highest court for decades to come."

To that accusation, we have a simple reply: "Boo-hoo, let's have a pity party!" Quite frankly, one of the fun things about winning the White House year in and year out is that we more or less own the Supreme Court, and if the Democrats don't like it they can put it where the sun don't shine.

Having said that, there's something to be learned from the Democrats' Supreme Court scare tactic. Why not rip a page from their playbook and energize our base by asking this question: What would the Supreme Court look like if the Democrats got their liberal mitts on it? Use the following doctored photo in your campaign mailings and watch those dollars come rolling in:

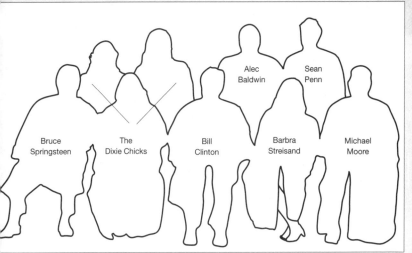

Bruce
Springsteen

The
Dixie Chicks

Bill
Clinton

Alec
Baldwin

Sean
Penn

Barbra
Streisand

Michael
Moore

MANIPULATING THE TERROR ALERT SYSTEM FOR MAXIMUM IMPACT

Most Americans are under the impression that the nation's color-coded terror alert system was created in March of 2002 by the Department of Homeland Security to alert the public to possible terrorist threats. In actuality, the system was devised by White House political advisor Karl Rove and a top-flight cadre of marketing executives for the purpose of manipulating public opinion and election results. While the color-coded system has accomplished next to nothing in terms of preparing the American people for a catastrophic attack, it has been undeniably effective in convincing the public that the only way to be truly safe in this age of global terror is by voting Republican.

Like other weapons in our political arsenal, like attack ads, talk radio, and Sean Hannity, the terror alert system must be used carefully in order to achieve maximum political impact. Switch the threat levels too often and the public may become confused; switch them too infrequently and the public may feel complacent or, worst of all, safe. Remember, a sense of safety and well-being in the voting public has traditionally been the Republican Party's worst enemy.

A review of the terror alert chart (*opposite page*) will show which situations dictate which threat levels in the system:

HOMELAND SECURITY ADVISORY SYSTEM

SEVERE
Hillary Leading In Polls

HIGH
Cheney Indicted

ELEVATED
Colin Powell Publishes Damaging Tell-All Memoir

GUARDED
Embarrassing New DeLay Revelations

LOW
GOP Leading Comfortably In House, Senate Races

Target:
HOWARD DEAN

After a disappointing showing in the 2004 Iowa caucuses, the former Vermont governor let loose with the now-legendary "Dean Scream," cementing his status as one of the monumental boobs in Democrat Party history. Here at the RNC, many of us wondered how Dr. Demento would be made to pay for his unhinged outburst, and on February 12, 2005, we got our answer: He was named head of the Democratic National Committee.

Some of us wondered whether this was the Democrats' idea of a practical joke. Others theorized that they only chose Dean because other excellent choices, like Pauly Shore and Carrot Top, were unavailable. Any way you slice it, though, one thing is for sure: Having Howard Dean as the official spokesman of the Democrat Party is the gift that keeps on giving!

How can we take advantage of this historic opportunity that the Democrats have handed us on a liberal platter? Simple: Every chance we get, we should use tactics that will cause Dean to blow his stack once more, preferably in the presence of TV cameras and microphones. The following is just a partial list of dirty tricks guaranteed to get Howard Dean really mad, but feel free to come up with your own—it's easy and it's really, really fun!

◎ When Howard Dean has to give a speech at a big rally, bribe the sound man to mess with the microphone so that every time Dean opens his mouth, the hall is filled with the ear-splitting squeal of feedback. Dean will be forced to put aside the microphone and shout at the crowd at the top of his lungs—and that's the footage that the cable news networks will run on a nonstop loop.

◎ Sneak into Democrat Party headquarters and substitute page 3 of Howard Dean's standard fundraising speech with an alphabetical list of the states. Odds are that Dean will make it all the way down to Idaho before he realizes something's up, and then watch that vein in his forehead go bananas!

◎ When Howard Dean is scheduled to make an appearance before the Council on Foreign Relations, sneak onto the stage and put a thumbtack on his chair. When he sits down on it, get ready for the simmering volcano known as Mt. Howard to erupt!

▲

Lesson

1

Iraq

As instructive as the previous chapters of *The Republican Playbook* have been, sometimes the best way to learn how to be a Republican is by example—in other words, by studying the work of a historical figure whose agility, deftness, and deviousness are an inspiration to us all. To this end, President Richard M. Nixon was a student of the lives of Niccolò Machiavelli, John Dillinger, and Attila the Hun. Similarly, today's generation of Republicans would be well advised to steep themselves in the ongoing legacy of President George W. Bush.

In the George W. Bush Leadership Series, we will revisit some of the great moments of the president's first five years in office, accomplishments that did not receive the coverage they deserved in the liberal–biased, gay marriage–loving media. In lesson one, we will take a look at how the president tackled one of the biggest challenges of his presidency: how to achieve victory in Iraq.

BUSH CALLS "PLAN FOR VICTORY" SLOGAN A SUCCESS
Vows to Create Additional Slogans to Defeat Insurgents

One day after making a speech on Iraq at the United States Naval Academy in front of a giant placard reading "Plan For Victory," President George W. Bush pronounced the "Plan For Victory" slogan an unqualified success.

"Much time, thought, and effort went into creating the 'Plan For Victory' slogan," Mr. Bush said today at a White House press conference. "I think we can all agree that the hard work that went into that slogan has really paid off."

The president said that not only were the words "Plan For Victory" catchy and memorable, but the choice of yellow letters against a blue background was perfect: "The yellow against the blue really made the letters stand out in a victory-like way."

Mr. Bush told reporters that he believed that "time and patience" were the ultimate keys to success in Iraq, adding, "It took time and patience for us to come up with a really effective slogan like 'Plan For Victory.'"

But even as he praised his administration's latest slogan, Mr. Bush said he would not rest on his laurels, vowing to create additional slogans to defeat the insurgents in Iraq.

"The insurgents may have many weapons at their disposal, but they are not as good as we are at coming up with slogans," Mr. Bush said. "So far the only one they've come up with is 'Jihad'—not catchy at all, if you ask me."

NEW VOTING BOOTH DESIGNS FOR HEAVILY DEMOCRAT DISTRICTS

The Republican Party believes and has always believed that in order to have a strong, thriving democracy, every vote cast by every voter must be counted. The validity and the credibility of the voting process must be safeguarded at all times, and any attempt to falsify, adulterate, or otherwise alter the results of a free democratic election must be strictly prohibited and, if found out, severely punished.

The preceding paragraph refers to the Republican Party's position on elections in Iraq. As for elections in the United States, our policy remains what it has always been: Elections are made to be stolen, by any means possible. And when it comes to stealing elections, we consider our efforts in recounting, miscounting, and not counting at all to be the gold standard in election fraud.

The 2000 Florida recount still reigns as our most shining moment, but it also set off alarm bells at GOP headquarters. We were able to win the Florida battle, thanks to our Election-Fixing Delta Strike Force led by James A. Baker III, but what if simultaneous election battlefields opened up across the country, in states like Ohio, Illinois, and California? Until there is a James A. Baker III robot capable of being several places at the same time, we will need another solution. (At press time, the James A. Baker III robot is not expected to be fully operational until 2012. An early prototype of the robot was sent back to the shop for re-engineering after it was found that it did not talk fast enough and left a telltale oil stain everywhere it went.)

Fortunately, technology has provided us with another way to get the vote counts we desire in heavily Democrat districts. Here are four newly designed voting booths we intend to smuggle into polling places in time for the upcoming election:

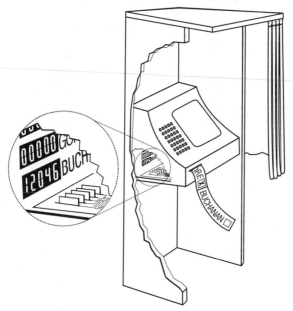

THE INACCUTRON™ 450

The Inaccutron™ 450 has the look and feel of a normal voting booth, and gives the voter the impression that it is registering the vote for the candidate of his choice. But thanks to state-of-the-art digital technology, no matter who the voter votes for, the Inaccutron™ casts a vote for Pat Buchanan.

continues on following page

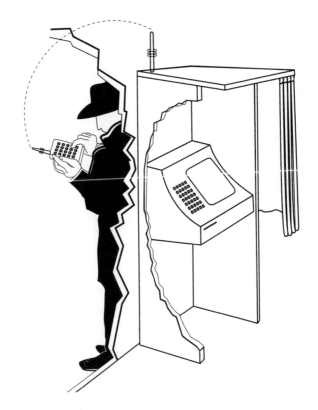

**THE RESULTSPRO
WITH EASYHACK™**

Finally, an electronic voting booth that voters find user-friendly, but that Republican operatives outside the polling place can hack into via a tiny, easily concealed remote-control radio device. Batteries not included.

Idea: combination voting machine/ATM to buy votes. Ask Mr. Cheney if this is legal.

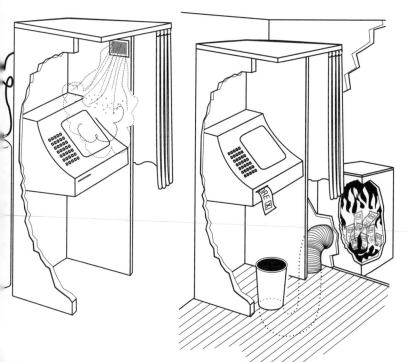

SLEEPYTIME™ VOTE MINIMIZER

You can't vote if you're unconscious, and that's the principle behind the Sleepytime™ Vote Minimizer. Moments after the voter enters the booth, wafer-thin gas vents release a thin mist of nitrous oxide, sending the voter crumbling to the ground—and sending his vote to Slumberland.

PAPER-NO-MOR BALLOTCINERATOR™

Worried about a pesky "paper trail" that might come back to haunt you if the Democrats demand a recount? Those worries are a thing of the past thanks to the Paper-No-Mor Ballotcinerator™. A trapdoor feature in the back of the voting mechanism drops paper records of votes cast into a gas-powered inferno hidden securely underneath the floor. With a state-of-the-art voting booth like this, who needs Katherine Harris?

SIX DEGREES OF HILLARY CLINTON

S en. Hillary Clinton's been making a serious move to the center over the past few years, supporting the troops, proposing a statute banning flag burning, and generally acting like . . .

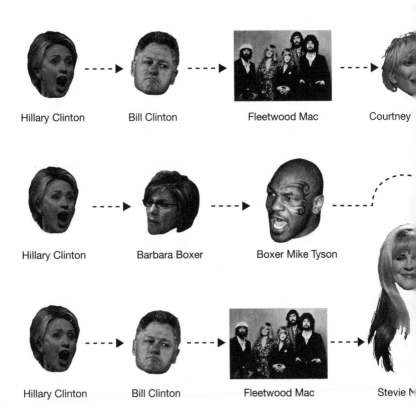

Hillary Clinton   Bill Clinton   Fleetwood Mac   Courtney

Hillary Clinton   Barbara Boxer   Boxer Mike Tyson

Hillary Clinton   Bill Clinton   Fleetwood Mac   Stevie N

one of us. Well, not so fast, Senator Centrist! To us you'll always be Mrs. Slick Willie, and these handy visual aids will help remind the voters who your real friends are:

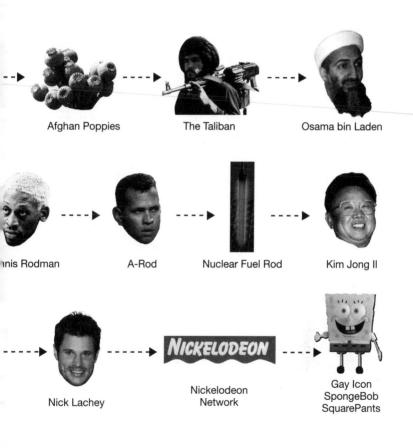

Afghan Poppies

The Taliban

Osama bin Laden

nis Rodman

A-Rod

Nuclear Fuel Rod

Kim Jong Il

Nick Lachey

Nickelodeon Network

Gay Icon SpongeBob SquarePants

DIRTY TRICK: PUSH POLLING

Every election year the Republican Party uses two different kinds of polling techniques: scientific polling and so-called push polling. In scientific polling, a carefully selected sample of voters is asked whether they approve of the job the president is doing. Those numbers are then calculated to within a margin of error of three percentage points, giving us an accurate idea of just how wildly we will later have to inflate those numbers to make the president appear to be doing well.

Push polling is a horse of a different color. In push polling, a Republican Party worker posing as a public-opinion pollster calls an unsuspecting voter and uses the pretext of "taking a poll" as a means of spreading scurrilous misinformation about a Democrat candidate. It's inexpensive, effective, and surprisingly fun. Try it once—we guarantee you, you'll be hooked!

The following script is an example of how push polling works. Use it as a general guideline, but as in all dirty tricks, what will work best for you are the sleazy maneuvers that you yourself come up with.

CALLER: Hello, do you have a few minutes to answer some questions about House minority leader Nancy Pelosi?

VOTER: Sure.

CALLER: I'm going to read some of her recent statements, and please tell me whether you strongly agree, agree, somewhat agree, somewhat disagree, disagree, or strongly disagree. Okay?

VOTER: Got it.

CALLER: Here's her first statement: "Illegal immigrants should be allowed to swarm over our borders and steal American jobs at will."

VOTER: Wait a - when did she say that?

CALLER: Last week, on the floor of the House. Do you strongly agree, agree -

VOTER: Strongly disagree.

CALLER: Okay, next statement: "American schoolchildren do not have easy enough access to pornography, and taxpayer dollars should be spent to make sure they do."

VOTER: (upset) Are you kidding me?! She actually said that?

CALLER: Do you strongly agree, agree...

VOTER: Strongly disagree! But really, she sounds like - I don't know, like she's on drugs or something...

CALLER: Next statement: "The only way to deal with cat overpopulation in this country is by drowning cute kittens at birth." Do you strongly agree, agree...

TALKING POINTS
Intelligent Design

This election year, Democrats are planning to try to put us on the defensive about the teaching of intelligent design in schools, claiming that the theory of evolution is science but intelligent design is not. Don't let them! The following talking points will shred the theory of evolution and dump it into the dustbin of history, along with such other crackpot theories as the theory of quantum mechanics and the theory of gravity.

- According to the theory of evolution, one of our direct ancestors was a creature called "homo erectus." You didn't have to grow up on Brokeback Mountain to know what that means. Teaching evolution is the Democrats' stealth way of telling our children that they are gay and their parents are gay, too, because we are all descendants of hairy gay apes. The Republican Party is the party of the Intelligent Designer; the Democrat Party is the party of the Interior Designer.

- The theory of evolution could not possibly exist because it can't be seen. The Democrats deny the existence of Saddam Hussein's weapons of mass destruction because no one has ever seen them, and yet they want to drum into our children a so-called scientific theory that is equally invisible. Hypocritical? Just a little bit! Our tax dollars should only go toward teaching children about things that can actually be seen, like the Holy Ghost.

■ Question: If man could evolve from apes, who's to say that at some point in the future the process might not be reversed, and apes might start evolving from man? The *Planet of the Apes* movies provide us with a chilling look at this doomsday scenario. Only one party wants a race of evil, superintelligent apes to enslave us: the Democrat Party.

■ There is a fine line between "scientist" and "Scientologist." Would you want Tom Cruise put in charge of teaching your children? How about Kirstie Alley? We didn't think so!

■ Put the pieces of a Mr. Potato Head together: That's what you get when an Intelligent Designer is at work. Now put those same pieces together in a bag, shake them up, and see what happens. Result? Evolution. Case closed!

PAYING FOR FAKE NEWSPAPER STORIES:
A BEGINNER'S GUIDE

It's been said that "freedom isn't free." The same can be said of a so-called "free" press. When it comes to what journalists choose to write for their newspapers, you truly do "get what you pay for." Left to their own devices, newspaper writers will fill endless column inches with facts and statistics, and nothing could be more confusing to the average voter at the height of a political campaign. In order to get at the truth, we must cut through that thicket of facts, and the only way to do that is by getting journalists to write what we tell them, and the only way to do that is by paying them, preferably in unmarked dollar bills.

Are there moral or ethical problems with paying for favorable press coverage? We looked into it, and here's the good news: There aren't. Of course, since we just wrote that particular piece of news, there's no way of knowing whether it's true or not.

But from a purely logical standpoint, by paying for fake news stories you are doing the average newspaper reader an enormous favor. Look at it this way: If a reader spends fifty cents on his daily newspaper, what would he rather read, a bunch of junk that was written for free, or expensive, hand-crafted works of fiction produced by a well-oiled political party machine? Clearly, the latter is giving him much more bang for his newspaper buck. So don't wring your hands over planting fake newspaper stories: The average reader would thank you for doing it, if he knew you were doing it.

Fortunately, most journalists are more than willing to be paid to write what you tell them to. Most of these ink-stained wretches have substantial gambling debts or alimony bills, and those that don't usually will accept payment in liquor.

The key to a successful planted news story, of course, is credibility. The minute the public suspects that we are paying to place these items, the jig is up. The following are four examples of newspaper stories we placed last year that no one suspected were untrue:

U.S. WINNING WAR ON OBESITY, SAYS CHENEY

What! No Vodka?

SHORT-SLEEVE SHIRT MANUFACTURERS PRAISE GLOBAL WARMING

In Closely Watched Sale, New Jersey's Utilities to Pay

itated toward auction programs loosely modeled on the New Jersey method.
The average price in this year's tion, announced yeste per kilo

POLL: REPEAL OF INHERITANCE TAX IS AMERICANS' NUMBER ONE CONCERN

Soar at State Auction

RIM Says It Has

'MY BAD,' SAYS CINDY SHEEHAN

Hunter Released From Ho

GEORGE W. BUSH NAMED SEXIEST MAN ALIVE

INFILTRATING THE DEMOCRATS:
DOS AND DON'TS

In 1972, President Richard M. Nixon ordered a team of burglars to break into the Democratic National Committee headquarters in Washington, D.C., to steal the Democrats' plans for the upcoming election. While this burglary and the subsequent cover-up became known as the Watergate scandal, the real scandal, from the Republican point of view, was how few plans worth stealing the Democrats actually had. After ransacking party headquarters, the best that the Watergate burglars could come up with was a cocktail napkin with the words "Nominate a Liberal" scrawled on it. All in all, such a "secret plan" hardly justified all the time, effort, and money we put into breaking into the place.

Over the years, the Democrats' plans for victory have gotten no more sophisticated ("Nominate a Liberal from Massachusetts" appears to be the latest incarnation), but our espionage techniques have grown by leaps and bounds. We no longer use such crude methods as burglary, but instead rely on high-tech listening devices and wiretapping technology developed by the Republican Party's sister organization, the National Security Agency (NSA). Sometimes, however, particularly at the local level, the best way to get information out of the Democrats is also one of the most old-fashioned dirty tricks in the book: infiltration. The Democrats are usually all too willing to welcome one of us into their sorry band, since they have been so thoroughly demoralized over the years that they are surprised, if not amazed, that anyone would actually want to become one of them. That's when the fun begins.

As easy as infiltration might sound at first blush, however, it is actually one of the most distasteful tasks around, because in order to be successful at it, you must actually look, sound, and act like a Democrat for hours at a time. Needless to say, this is not a task for the squeamish, and posing as a Democrat can cause unfortunate physical reactions such as unsightly rashes, hives, and projectile vomiting. With that caveat in mind, here are some Dos and Don'ts for posing as a Democrat:

DO pretend to listen to National Public Radio. This is a radio service that is available at the lower end of the FM dial that features an unappetizing stew of liberal-biased news, scratchy bluegrass recordings, and a supposedly entertaining automobile-repair program. In order to pass as a Democrat, you must be conversant in all NPR programming and be prepared to discuss it lovingly. This means you will have to sit through all of it, including a truly interminable show called *A Prairie Home Companion*. As we said before, this assignment is not for the squeamish.

DON'T let on that you have ever attended a NASCAR race. No Democrat has ever gone to NASCAR, and even the most casual mention of it will give you away. If the word "NASCAR" should somehow slip out and one of your Democrat "friends" asks what you said, reply, "I said the new film by Pedro Almodóvar."

DO walk around with slouched shoulders, shuffling your feet in a depressed manner. Remember, the Democrats have been going down to electoral defeat for years and as a result, they now lead lives of quiet desperation. When you show up at campaign headquarters, you should appear as though it took everything you had just to get out of bed in the morning. If you act in that cheerful, upbeat, I-just-got-a-dividend-tax-cut way, you'll instantly be branded as a Republican and the jig will be up.

DON'T wear a flag lapel pin. Remember, the Democrats want to burn all our flags. If you can somehow find a lapel pin of a flag on fire, wear that. Ladies, don't wear a brooch. Only Republican ladies wear brooches. Also, never refer to yourself as "ladies." There is no such thing as a Democrat lady.

COMMON DEMOCRAT EXPRESSIONS

The only thing I like better than taxing is spending.

As far as I'm concerned, we can never have enough lesbians teaching our children.

I saw Osama bin Laden's last video and you know what? He made a lot of good points.

If you ask me, we should ban the Bible and legalize heroin.

Democrats SUCK.

. . . that Abraham Lincoln wasn't gay, after all? For the past few years, Democrat historians have made a concerted effort to portray our great Republican president, Honest Abe, as Honestly Fabulous Abe. It's all a part of their conspiracy to advance their gay agenda by turning one of our Republican icons into a stovepipe hat–wearing nancy boy. They've even trotted out the facts that Abraham Lincoln shared a bed with another man, Joshua Fry Speed, for four years and wrote love letters to him. Proof that Lincoln was gay? Hardly. The fact is, Honest Abe was working as an undercover homosexual to "out" real gays like Speed, whom Lincoln later turned in to the proper authorities. At least that's the story we're going with.

SCARE TACTIC:
SOCIAL SECURITY

Nothing gets voters to the voting booths faster than scaring the bejesus out of them, and nothing scares the bejesus out of them better than the prospect that Social Security is running out of money. Tell them that they're going to lose their Social Security checks and voters become like lab chimps glued to electrodes, ready to do your bidding at the slightest jolt. Is Social Security running out of money? We haven't checked, so don't ask us. But for the purposes of winning elections, let's just say it is, and let that be our little secret.

How easy is it to convince voters that Social Security is going belly-up? Let's put it this way: If we could convince them that a couple of broken-down old vans in Iraq were "mobile chemical-weapons labs," selling them our little story about Social Security's insolvency should be a slam dunk. The key is to come up with a good round-numbered year when Social Security will go under: 2030, 2040, 2050, etc. That makes it sound like you've really done the research and you know what you're talking about. The older the audience you're speaking to, the sooner the year should be. We don't want the old bastards to think they have any breathing room.

When making your case, use a lot of numbers, and the more numbers, the better. Thanks to our educational system, very few Americans have command over simple addition and subtraction, let alone the kind of intentionally confusing math that is a hallmark of every good Republican Social Security speech.

In the past, we've urged Americans to invest their Social Security money in the stock market, thus funneling even more money to brokers and investment bankers, who, as the richest .0001 percent of Americans, represent the Republican base. So far, the Democrats in Congress have prevented us from privatizing Social Security in this manner (losers!), so this election cycle we intend to go over their heads and ask the voters to send their Social Security contributions directly to Vice President Dick Cheney. As the following graph shows, in good times and bad, Dick Cheney has outperformed both the Social Security trust fund and the S&P 500. In fact, with an 80 percent annual return, the only investment vehicle that has outperformed Dick Cheney is Ahmed Chalabi.

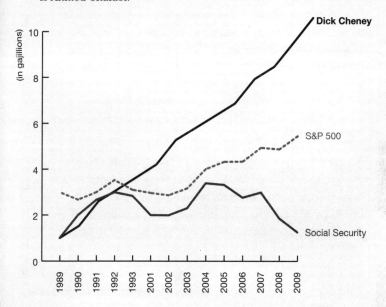

TALKING POINTS

Torture

All of a sudden, thanks to liberal politicians and pundits, "torture" has become a dirty word in America. While it is fashionable to call torture "un-American," any student of American society knows that just the opposite is true. A quick look at the facts shows that nothing, we repeat, nothing, is more American than torture.

Here's an example. Have you been to the Department of Motor Vehicles lately to renew your driver's license, or perhaps pick up some new license plates for your Ford Explorer? If you have, you were probably subjected to endless lines, waiting, and poor service when your number was eventually called. Some would call this an inconvenience, but we have another word for it: torture. That's right, torture. And not only is it torture, but it is torture carried out by the government, on its citizens. Has the American Civil Liberties Union made a stink about the DMV? Why, no, they're too busy defending homosexuals' right to teach our children how to have sex.

So, clearly, a double standard is at work here. So-called human rights groups and professional crybabies like Jimmy Carter love to complain about Iraqis being dragged around by a leash at Abu Ghraib, but when it comes to John Q. Taxpayer being tortured while trying to exercise his constitutional right to drive an

SUV, it's jake with them. They shouldn't call them Democrats—they should call them Hypocrats.

Even though it is obvious that torture is a part of the glorious fabric of American life, on the campaign trail you will probably be subjected to some tough questions regarding our party's position on torture, especially if your advance team fails to weed out the malcontents in your town hall audience. Just in case, keep in mind these talking points.

- The United States never uses any interrogation techniques that have not been widely used in the past, e.g., during the Spanish Inquisition.

- If terror suspects don't want to be held indefinitely without being charged, why don't they just admit they were trying to blow up something? Talk about torture—it's torture waiting for these jerks to confess.

- When the United States transports terror suspects to other countries in order to be interrogated—the process known as "rendition"—the government gives them frequent-flier miles. Through this program, known as Terror Rewards™, terror suspects can earn valuable premiums such as travel to Hawaii, the Caribbean, and much, much more.

ALL-PURPOSE FOLKSY ANECDOTE TEMPLATE™

During his eight years in the White House, President Ronald Reagan frequently punctuated his speeches with heart-warming, folksy anecdotes that touched on real people and their real concerns. Years later, many of these anecdotes turned out to be exaggerated or, in some cases, totally made up. All this proves is that the "Great Communicator" knew something that Republicans have known for years: Real people can be a real pain to talk to, because they don't always say what you want them to say. Year in, year out, experience shows that the most effective true-life anecdotes are the ones that never happened.

Since 1985, the Republican Party has relied exclusively on the All-Purpose Folksy Anecdote Template™ to generate the sort of heart-tugging stories necessary to make GOP politicians appear to care about ordinary people, or even to have met them. We guarantee that by using the Template, your approval numbers among women voters will skyrocket faster than you can say "soccer mom." Hello, Folksy Anecdote Template—good-bye, gender gap!

FOLKSY ANECDOTE TEMPLATE

The other night I had the best slice of pizza I've ever had at

_____. And while I was there I got a chance to meet
LOCAL PIZZA PARLOR

_____, who was taking her son _____
ETHNIC-SOUNDING FEMALE NAME   BOY'S NAME

and his soccer team out for some pizza after a game. And

_____ said to me, "_____, could you please tell
MOTHER'S NAME   (YOUR NAME HERE)

the Democrats in Washington that instead of worrying about

things like gay marriage and _____, we want
                                          OTHER LIBERAL ISSUE

Congress to focus on the things that are important to us right

here in _____?" And I said, "Well, _____,
          LOCAL TOWN   MOTHER'S NAME

like what?" And she said, "Like giving a tax cut to the richest one

percent of Americans. That way, the money trickles down to all

of us ordinary folks right here in _____." Well,
                                        LOCAL TOWN

_____, I don't know if you're listening to me right
MOTHER'S NAME

now, but I'm going to take your message back with me to those

liberal Democrats in Washington. Because not only does

_____ have the best pizza in the world—it has the best
LOCAL TOWN

people, too. (APPLAUSE)

THE FOG OF WAR:
HOW TO CREATE IT

Much has been made of the fact that both President George W. Bush and Vice President Dick Cheney avoided serving in the Vietnam War. Here at the Republican National Committee, we believe that the draft-dodging of these two great men only speaks to their great political acumen. Rather than serving in the military at a time when such service could do nothing for their approval ratings, they waited until they were powerful enough to invade countries, thus reaping the benefits of the so-called "rally 'round the flag" phenomenon. The fact is, waging war can be a big boost to the popularity of the party in power, since anyone who disagrees with the war can be accused of not "supporting the troops." Whoever said that "war is hell" clearly never sat in on our focus groups. If you spin it right, war is sweet.

But that's a big "if." One of the many downsides of having a free press is that in times of war, they have an annoying tendency to report bad news, often about things being blown up and people being killed and wounded. That is why it is our job to ensure that the news coming out of Iraq in the months going forward is as good as possible, or, failing that, incredibly confusing.

Fortunately, confusing the American people about the actual status of the war is extremely easy. With the aid of several top Pentagon officials, we have put together the following easy-to-follow guide to making the fog of war thicker than ever:

- **TALK ENDLESSLY ABOUT THE SHIITES, SUNNIS, AND KURDS.** There are three principal factions in Iraq, and luckily for us, most Americans cannot distinguish one from the other. The more you sprinkle your speeches with frequent references to the Shiites, Sunnis, and Kurds, the harder it will be for people to follow your train of thought. Ditto for those tricky, impossible-to-tell-apart Arab names. How many voters can tell the difference between Abu Musab al-Zarqawi and Ayman al-Zawahiri? Not too many, we'll wager.

- **MASTER THE ART OF RUMSPEAK.** Next time Donald Rumsfeld gives a press briefing, pay close attention. Marvel at the circumlocution, the double negatives, the totally made-up words. Then try it yourself, and be careful to use meaningless phrases like "not knowable." Tip: When you yourself no longer understand what you are saying, you have learned to speak like the master.

- **WHEN THE ENEMY SUCCEEDS, CALL THEM "DESPERATE."** This never fails. When the enemy pulls off a successful attack, spin it by saying that their success is only proof of how desperate they have become. This means the more the enemy wins, the more they lose. Confused? Mission accomplished!

DIRTY TRICK:
FUN WITH WIKIPEDIA

As Republicans, we have always embraced new technology in our tireless search for innovative and creative ways to commit character assassination on our opponents. The advent of radio and television enabled us to spread lies about Democrats, their voting records, and their unhealthy sexual interest toward their pets to audiences far larger than in the olden days, when we would drive up and down the street in a van with a megaphone. But in the twenty-first century, the technology of radio and television seem positively Stone Age compared to the greatest smear-distribution system known to man: the Internet.

We're not talking about "blogs." While blogs are widely assumed to be powerful, that is just another one of those urban myths, like the one about tobacco being bad for you. As of this writing, there are over 20.6 million bloggers in America, and their collective output is read by a total of only four hundred people, all of them media critics who have their own blogs that no one reads. No, when we talk about the character-assassination potential of the Internet, we are thinking of one website and one website alone: Wikipedia.

Wikipedia bills itself as the free encyclopedia "that anyone can edit," which, loosely translated, means "that anyone with a computer can add anything to without worrying that anyone will ever check to see if it's true or not." When we first learned about Wikipedia here at RNC headquarters, we were like kids in a candy store, and immediately logged on and started burnishing to perfection the biographies of our favorite Democrats. The following are some particularly lively examples of our Wikipedia handiwork:

Harry Reid

Harry Mason Reid (born December 2, 1939) is the senior United States senator from Nevada and a member of the Democrat Party, for which he serves as Senate minority leader. Before Senator Reid gained prominence as a political figure, however, he was best known as one of the most successful and prolific porn stars in America. Going by the name of Harry Rod, he scored an early hit in 1983 with *Flashpants (Cop a Feeling)*, demonstrating an athleticism and feral sexuality that endeared him to even the most discerning porn consumer . . .

Joseph R. Biden

Joseph Robinette "Joe" Biden Jr. (born November 20, 1942) is an American lawyer and politician from Wilmington, Delaware, in New Castle County. He is a member of the Democrat Party and is the incumbent senior U.S. senator from Delaware. In his tenure in the Senate, he has grabbed headlines by sponsoring a series of controversial bills, including 1991's Crackpipes for Kids initiative which would have distributed free crackpipes to all of America's schoolchildren . . .

John Reid Edwards

John Reid Edwards (born June 10, 1953) is an American attorney and politician from the U.S. state of North Carolina. A Democrat, Edwards was indicted in January of 2006 for murdering the legendary rapper Tupac Shakur . . .

Good use of the Internets!!!

FOREWORD
to the 1972 Edition

By President Richard M. Nixon

*I*n 1972, President Richard M. Nixon commissioned the first
Republican Playbook, *and thus realized a long-standing
dream of his: to put all of his favorite political dirty tricks
between the covers of a book. Always mindful of his place in history, Nixon felt the* Playbook *would someday serve as a monu-
ment to his political genius, and so he assembled a world-class
brain trust to assemble the book, including top advisors from
the Nixon, Eisenhower, and Stalin administrations.*

*The following is Nixon's foreword to the 1972 edition. While
some of the advice in it may now seem slightly outdated, the
foreword has been included in every edition of the* Playbook *for
its historical interest, and also as a tribute to this great, if somewhat misunderstood, man.*

For years, my enemies have relished calling me "Tricky Dick."
The ironic thing is that I actually love that nickname. Any visi-
tor to the Oval Office can attest to that, since right there on the
sofa is a pillow that Pat made for me with "Tricky Dick" needle-
pointed on it. To me, being called "tricky" is the highest compliment a politician can ever receive, and I hope that this book will
serve as testimony to just how tricky this Dick can be.

Before you read this book, and take advantage of my decades
of experience in skullduggery, chicanery, and sabotage, here are
a few words of wisdom from Tricky Dick himself:

- When planning a burglary, conspiracy, or cover-up, always be sure to tape-record all of your conversations. This will serve as a valuable historical record and will never come back to haunt you.

- Always keep an extensive "enemies list" of people you intend to wiretap or otherwise harass using all the agencies of the government that are at your imperial disposal. It will help you keep a running tally of the people who are out to get you, and no one will ever find out about its existence.

- If you intend to abuse your power in ways that clearly violate the United States Constitution, it is important that you only confide in people who can be trusted not to talk to the press. In my case, I have been blessed with many such trusted advisors, including people like FBI agent Mark Felt.

With those helpful tips in mind, and if you follow the advice in this *Playbook*, I have no doubt that Republicans will occupy the White House for another four-year term. Spiro and I look forward to serving each and every day of it.

TRICKY DICK

REPUBLICAN EXCEPTIONS TO THE TEN COMMANDMENTS

In order to pander to our evangelical base, it is very important to refer to the Ten Commandments in speeches and to defend the right of those who wish to post them in front of courthouses and other public buildings. As a practical matter,

I.
"I AM THE LORD THY GOD, WHO BROUGHT THEE OUT OF THE LAND OF EGYPT, OUT OF THE HOUSE OF BONDAGE. THOU SHALT HAVE NO OTHER GODS BEFORE ME."
Exception: In any direct conflict between God and Dick Cheney, Dick Cheney wins.

II.
"THOU SHALT NOT MAKE FOR THYSELF A GRAVEN IMAGE, OR ANY LIKENESS OF ANYTHING THAT IS IN HEAVEN ABOVE, OR THAT IS IN THE EARTH BENEATH, OR THAT IS IN THE WATER UNDER THE EARTH; THOU SHALT NOT BOW DOWN TO THEM OR SERVE THEM."
Exception: It is perfectly acceptable to bow down to the gun and tobacco industries, as well as certain defense contractors.

III.
"THOU SHALT NOT TAKE THE NAME OF THE LORD THY GOD IN VAIN; FOR THE LORD WILL NOT HOLD HIM GUILTLESS WHO TAKES HIS NAME IN VAIN."
Exception: The phrases "Those goddamn liberals" and "That goddamn Barbra Streisand" are perfectly all right.

IV.
"REMEMBER THE SABBATH DAY, TO KEEP IT HOLY. SIX DAYS THOU SHALT LABOR, AND DO ALL THY WORK; BUT THE SEVENTH DAY IS A SABBATH TO THE LORD THY GOD; IN IT THOU SHALT NOT DO ANY WORK."
Exception: President Bush is allowed to clear brush on Sunday, but only because he makes up for it by not doing any work Monday through Saturday.

however, the Ten Commandments are nearly impossible to obey in the course of a bare-fisted political campaign and are in direct contradiction to almost every rule listed in this *Playbook*. To resolve this seeming contradiction, we have developed the following Republican Exceptions to the Ten Commandments, which should allow you as a Republican to go about your business hypocrisy-free.

V.
"HONOR THY FATHER AND THY MOTHER, THAT THY DAYS MAY BE LONG IN THE LAND WHICH THE LORD THY GOD GIVES THEE."
Exception: If your father did not march on Baghdad and depose Saddam because he didn't have "U.N. approval," you don't have to honor that wimpy decision.

VI.
"THOU SHALT NOT KILL."
Exception: Iraqis, Afghans, and President Hugo Chávez of Venezuela.

VII.
"THOU SHALT NOT COMMIT ADULTERY."
Exception for Newt Gingrich, Henry Hyde, etc.

VIII.
"THOU SHALT NOT STEAL."
Exception: Millions of dollars of kickbacks from Indian tribes paid to Republican lobbyists do not count.

IX.
"THOU SHALT NOT BEAR FALSE WITNESS AGAINST THY NEIGHBOR."
Exception: It's okay to let the Swift Boat Veterans for Truth do it.

X.
"THOU SHALT NOT COVET THY NEIGHBOR'S HOUSE; THOU SHALT NOT COVET THY NEIGHBOR'S WIFE, OR HIS MANSERVANT, OR HIS MAIDSERVANT, OR HIS OX, OR HIS ASS, OR ANYTHING THAT IS THY NEIGHBOR'S."
Exception: Petroleum.

†ALKING POINTS
Gay Cartoons

FACT: The Democrats will not rest until every person in the United States of America is gay. This has been an undisputable cornerstone of the Democrat agenda for some time, and there is a very simple electoral logic behind it. Since homosexuals tend to vote Democratic in overwhelming numbers, the Democrats have wisely reasoned that the more gays there are, the more votes for Democrat candidates. Therefore, they are putting their pedal to the metal to make all of us gay, as soon as possible.

A major tent pole of their plan has been a systematic attempt to insert gay culture into the mainstream of American life, so that people will gradually turn gay without even knowing what is happening to them. Through a secret financial network, the Democrats have underwritten everything from *Will and Grace* to *Queer Eye for the Straight Guy* to Elton John's marriage. But nowhere has their influence been more strongly pronounced than in their television programming targeting America's children: gay cartoons. By seducing America's youth with a broad array of lovable but swishy cartoon characters, the Democrats hope to raise an entire generation of gay, and therefore Democratic, voters. While the Democrats have traditionally been the party of gay cartoons that advocate the homosexual lifestyle, we Republicans have always supported ultraviolent cartoons that foster such traditional American values as gun ownership and pre-emptive invasion of foreign countries.

Much has been made in recent years of such flamingly gay characters as SpongeBob SquarePants, but Democrat-inspired gay cartoons have a long, storied past. Perhaps the longest-running and gayest cartoon series of all time is one that has remained safely under the radar: *The Flintstones*. "The Flintstones," you gasp. "I've enjoyed their antics for years—are you sure they're gay?" Consider these facts:

- Fred and Barney are inseparable, and are seen more frequently in each other's company than with their so-called wives, Betty and Wilma.

- Fred and Barney hail from the extremely gay-sounding town of "Bedrock."

- Fred and Barney are never shown wearing pants.

- The theme song of *The Flintstones* promises the viewer, "When you're with the Flintstones . . . you'll have a gay old time." The Democrats may approve of this sort of thing, but as Republicans, we yabba-dabba don't.

I like The Flintstones —
does that mean I am
gay? Ask Mr. Cheney.

DIRTY TRICK:
FUN WITH PHOTOSHOP

In the olden days, when Republicans wanted to embarrass Democrats in the heat of a political campaign, we used to have to dispatch photographers to trail them for days on end, hoping to catch them in a compromising situation. In some cases, it was a huge waste of time and we came up empty; in other cases, like that of Gary Hart, it barely took a day and it was like winning Powerball. But the era of shadowing Democrats with a camera and a telephoto lens are long gone, thanks to a magnificent innovation of the digital age known as Photoshop. Through the wonders of Photoshop technology, compromising photos of Democrats are just a point and a click away, ready for mass distribution on the Internet (thank you, Al Gore)!

Here are some examples of the wonders Photoshop can do:

John Kerry testifying before
Congress becomes . . .

John Kerry in front of
the North Vietnamese flag.

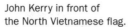

Donald Rumsfeld shaking hands
with Saddam becomes . . .

John Kerry shaking hands
with Saddam.

Kate Moss allegedly
snorting cocaine becomes . . .

John Kerry allegedly
snorting cocaine.

HOW TO BREEZE THROUGH CONFIRMATION HEARINGS WHILE SAYING PRACTICALLY NOTHING AT ALL

The United States Constitution dictates that when the President nominates someone to the Supreme Court or cabinet, it is the United States Senate's job to "advise and consent." Similarly, *The Republican Playbook* dictates that when a nominee is brought before the Senate for confirmation hearings, it is that nominee's responsibility to "disguise and pretend." That means that regardless of the fact that you have passed the Republican litmus test with flying colors and have sworn to oppose abortion, gun control, and the teaching of science in our schools, when you appear in front of a Senate committee for your confirmation hearing you must "disguise" those beliefs and "pretend" to believe absolutely nothing at all.

Unfortunately, this is easier said than done. Confirmation hearings are designed by the Senate Democrats to be as intimidating as possible, and could very well be the most terrifying experience of your life, next to the naked wrestling part of your Skull and Bones initiation. At a Senate Judiciary Committee confirmation, for example, the room will be packed with TV cameras, blinding lights, and Teddy Kennedy's enormous, terrifying head. But don't let those things shake you. You're a Republican, and when the going gets tough, Republicans say nothing.

That doesn't mean, however, that you can just sit there and zip your piehole. The Democrats and their lackeys at National

That was Awesome!

Public Radio and *The NewsHour with Jim Lehrer* will expect you to say something, and taking the Fifth at your own confirmation hearing tends not to make the right impression. Therefore, your best bet is to use the following all-purpose confirmation hearing answers, *regardless of the questions you are asked*:

- Senator, I believe it is the inalienable right of every American to own pets. Based on my reading of the Constitution, I believe that the framers felt that this country was founded on the principle that citizens could take ownership of cats and dogs as well as goldfish, if they desire, and if confirmed I will tirelessly defend that right.

- Senator, I firmly believe that there are fifty states in this country, including Alaska and Hawaii, and I am strongly in favor of this being taught in our nation's schools.

- Senator, in answer to your question about *Roe v. Wade*, I would like to say that Wade has one more letter in it than Roe, but other than that I haven't looked into the issue seriously enough to state an opinion on it at this time.

- In terms of stem cell research, I would like to say that I live at 4356 Hillcrest Road in Bethesda, Maryland.

REPUBLICAN CHILDREN'S BOOKS: UPCOMING RELEASES

At the Republican National Committee, our motto is the same as America's leading cigarette manufacturers: "Get them while they're young." Lynne V. Cheney, Vice President Dick Cheney's wife, knows this better than anybody, having penned three highly regarded children's books, all with a not-so-hidden agenda: By getting America's children "hooked" on the Republican "habit," they will someday grow up to be Republican voters, ready to oppose gay marriage and support domestic spying.

With that in mind, we at the RNC have commissioned several leading Republican politicians to write GOP-themed books specifically for America's children. While the propaganda value of these delightful books may not be reaped for some time to come, it should kick in around the time of the 2032 election, when Barb and Jenna Bush will be running for president and vice-president, respectively.

See about getting Cliff's Notes to these →

THE SMITH AND WESSON THAT COULD
By Sen. Rick Santorum (R-Penn.)

This inspirational volume tells the tale of Rifey, a Smith and Wesson rifle who couldn't shoot bullets at all, because mean gun-control advocates said he couldn't . . . until one day, when Rifey gets bought at a gun show with no background checks. Then it's Rifey's chance to show the world just what he's made  of, going on a shooting spree across seven Southern states!

HARRY REID AND THE CHAMBER OF TEDIUM
By Sen. Bill Frist (R-Tenn.)

Who is Harry Reid? Wizard? Warlock? No, just an extremely tedious man who casts a sleeping spell over a room of one hundred men and women with his astonishingly boring speeches!

MAKE WAY FOR DRILLING
By Sen. Ted Stevens (R-Alaska)

Set in the Arctic National Wildlife Refuge, this is the charming story of a mama puffin and her six babies who must cross a perilous terrain of oil derricks, pipelines, and construction vehicles as they run for their lives. Warning: Contains graphic scenes, including one in which a baby puffin is crushed to death by a Hummer.

PROPOSE A BOGUS
CONSTITUTIONAL AMENDMENT

Are you a student of the United States Constitution? Most Republicans are, except for the ones who get nominated to the Supreme Court. Well, if you're interested in the Constitution, then these facts may be of interest to you:

Number of amendments to the Constitution ratified since 1789:
27

Number of amendments to the Constitution proposed by Republican political candidates since 2002:
40,391

As the statistics above would seem to suggest, it is a lot easier to propose an amendment to the Constitution than to actually get an amendment ratified. Now, here's another interesting fact: Of the 40,391 amendments proposed by Republican candidates, zero, that's right, zero have been ratified. Does this mean Republicans are really bad at getting their amendments ratified? Not at all, for one simple reason: We never intended any of these amendments to make it into the Constitution in the first place!

That's right. When a Republican politician proposes a Constitutional amendment, it is for one reason and one reason only: to put the Democrats on the defensive. Whether it's an amendment banning flag burning or gay marriage, or an amendment protecting the right to pray in schools or inserting the word "God" in the Pledge of Allegiance, all of these bogus amendments serve the same purpose. Invariably, Democrats are forced to oppose the amendments, and then have a dickens of a time explaining their position to the voters. You haven't lived until you've seen the way a bogus Constitutional amendment makes a Democrat squirm.

So what do we at the Republican National Committee have in the bogus-constitutional-amendment pipeline? Try this on for size: a constitutional amendment banning the torturing of eagles. Here's how it'll play out. We'll propose the amendment in Congress. The Democrats will oppose it, claiming that there is no evidence that eagles are being tortured to begin with. That's all the red meat we need. Within milliseconds, we'll issue mass e-mails showing that the Democrats do not oppose the torturing of eagles, our national symbol. Within a day, our flunkies at Fox News will have made it their number one story. Within two days, the Democrats will be fielding angry calls from outraged constituents, and our campaign war chests will be brimming with fresh cash.

Sometimes being a Republican is just too easy.

REPUBLICAN-TO-ENGLISH GLOSSARY

As Republicans, we speak a language all our own. While this language resembles English in some superficial ways—alphabet, spelling, grammar—a closer examination of the Republican language reveals that when we Republicans say something, we rarely mean what English-speaking people think we mean. This is very useful to us, because it means that by using our own special language instead of English, we can mislead people without even breaking a sweat. Mastery of this language is invaluable, and it can be used in almost any setting: the stump speech, the televised debate, and most importantly, the presidential press conference. The more fluent you become in the Republican language, the harder it will be for anyone else to know what you are really saying—unless they, too, are fluent in Republican like you. Thus, the Republican language becomes like a dog whistle that only other Republicans can hear.

Having said that, speaking Republican is not easy. It takes years of study and practice, and even then, it is still possible for a Republican politician, at the end of a long day on the campaign trail, to "slip" and say what he really means in easy-to-understand English instead of impossible-to-penetrate Republican. To keep these regrettable mishaps from occurring, we have included the following facts-at-your-fingertips Republican-to-English Glossary. Give yourself a quick refresher course, and soon you'll be talking Republican like a pro!

REPUBLICAN	ENGLISH
Tax relief	Tax cut
Pro-life	Antiabortion
No Child Left Behind	Every Child Tested Up the Wazoo
Support our troops	Agree with our president
Axis of Evil	Axis of Oil
Personal responsibility	Welfare cuts
Family values	Heterosexuality
New York liberal	Jew
Feminist	Lesbo
A thousand points of light	A cardboard box over a subway grate
Kinder, gentler	Just as badass as before
My fellow Americans	My fellow evangelical Christians
I'm resigning to spend more time with my family.	I've been canned because an entire city was flooded while I sat on my ass.

▲
Lesson
2
The Environment

Critics of President George W. Bush often accuse him of having no environmental policy. Actually, his environmental policy is much better thought-out and more consistent than that of the so-called environmentalists who take such glee in attacking him. While his enemies in the Sierra Club or the World Wildlife Fund will arbitrarily label one species "endangered" and another "not endangered," President Bush resolutely refuses to play favorites. As long as he is president, every species on the planet is endangered.

Despite such a solid record on the environment, the president continues to draw fire from the tree-hugging left, particularly for backing out of the so-called Kyoto Protocol on global warming. On that issue, however, the president has not only been consistent but also intellectually rigorous, as the following archival news item demonstrates.

BUSH REAFFIRMS SUPPORT FOR GLOBAL WARMING

Makes Earth a 'Homier' Place, President Says

On the day that the U.N. Kyoto Protocol finally went into effect, President George W. Bush reaffirmed his strong support for global warming, arguing that the phenomenon helps to make the world a "toastier, homier" place.

"Right now, Hawaii has a climate that is the envy of the world," Mr. Bush said at a White House briefing. "If global warming continues at its current pace, by 2050 the whole world will be as hot as Hawaii, if not hotter."

President Bush added that global warming—far from being the threat to the world's ecosystem that many experts say it is—may actually be the best long-term solution to the world's energy problems.

"If the world got a few degrees warmer every year, we wouldn't have to turn up the darned thermostat so much," Mr. Bush said. "Thanks to global warming, the world will be a toastier, homier place."

Mr. Bush said that each and every American can do his or her part to help increase global warming, adding, "Instead of walking to the corner, drive your SUV."

"A lot of folks think they can't do much to produce greenhouse gases, but that's just not true," Mr. Bush said. "Every little bit helps."

ACCUSE THE DEMOCRATS OF FLIP-FLOPPING, EVEN IF THEY DIDN'T

"I actually did vote for the $87 billion before I voted against it."
— Sen. John Kerry (D-Mass.)

When we heard John Kerry say those immortal words during the 2004 campaign, we at the Republican National Committee fell off our chairs, then got down on our knees, then thanked the Almighty for creating the junior senator from Massachusetts. As the campaign wore on, John Kerry's mouth was the gift that kept on giving. Why? Because every time he opened it, he flip-flopped, and if there's one thing that the *Playbook* teaches us it is that accusing the Democrats of flip-flopping is a tactic that always works—whether they've actually flip-flopped or not.

In contrast with John Kerry, President George W. Bush has never flip-flopped in his life. Take Iraq, for example. He said that he was invading Iraq because Saddam Hussein possessed weapons of mass destruction. After there was substantial evidence that there were no weapons of mass destruction, he maintained that there were, and we just hadn't found them yet. Then, when it became clear that the claims about WMD were based on phony intelligence, he steadfastly said that he was right to invade Iraq, even if he did it for the wrong reason. The lesson in this is that the American people prefer someone who is consistently wrong to someone who flip-flops.

Of course, in John Kerry's case, we had on our hands the flip-flopping champion of the world, because he flip-flopped more than the doggy door of a cocker spaniel with a weak bladder. But Kerry was far from the first Democrat we accused of flip-flopping. Check out this quote from the first President Bush, running against Bill Clinton in 1992: "It's the White House, not the waffle house." So was Clinton the first Democrat we accused of flip-flopping? Wrong! In 1972, the year this *Playbook* was first published, President Nixon ran a series of TV ads showing a picture of Democratic nominee George McGovern, then reversing it horizontally, while a narrator accused him of—you guessed it—"flip-flopping."

You would think that sooner or later the American people would realize that we use the same flip-flopping charges in every election, regardless of the candidate, and regardless of how accurate the charges are. But they don't. Why? Because the average American watches over twenty-eight hours of television a week, which has succeeded in making him stupider and stupider from one election to the next. Which is why, here at the RNC, we say that a short attention span is a Republican's best friend.

OFFICIAL REPUBLICAN
SUPREME COURT LITMUS TEST

Whenever a Republican President introduces a new nominee to the United States Supreme Court, he always assures the press that the individual has not passed a "litmus test." The nominee, for his part, will vehemently say that he will abide by a strict reading of the United States Constitution and has never been asked to pass a "litmus test." Finally, while testifying before the Senate in his confirmation hearings, the nominee will swear up and down that no one has ever even *mentioned* to him the concept of a "litmus test."

With that in mind, it is our pleasure to present to you the Official Republican Supreme Court Litmus Test which all Republican candidates must pass to be nominated for the United States Supreme Court.

1) I believe that a woman has the right to
  a) choose
  b) party
  ~~c) vote~~
  d) protest outside abortion clinics

2) I believe that life begins
  a) in the first trimester
  b) in the second trimester
  ~~c) at conception~~
  d) when Pat Robertson says it begins

3) When I have some downtime, I like to

   a) watch TV

   b) read

   c) enjoy my hobbies

   d) think of ways to abolish abortion

4) I believe that the best birth control method is

   a) abortion

   b) the pill

   c) the "morning after" pill

   d) keeping a picture of Joan Rivers on
      your nightstand

5) If I am elected to the Supreme Court, I will

   a) preserve, protect, and defend the Constitution

   b) vigorously safeguard civil liberties

   c) steadfastly remain above politics

   d) be a panting lapdog of the religious Right

6) In the movie *Godzilla Vs. Megalon*,
   I rooted for

   a) Godzilla

   b) Megalon

   c) neither

   d) Wade

If you answered "d" to all of the above questions, con-gratulations—you have passed the Official Republican Supreme Court Litmus Test and are well on your way to becoming the next Antonin Scalia!

I rule !!!

LITMUS TEST ★ [79]

Target:
MICHAEL MOORE

Of the many persistent critics the Republican Party has had to endure over the past two decades, perhaps none is as irritating as author-slash-filmmaker Michael Moore. Opinionated, loudmouthed, and tubby, Moore is a fixture at every Academy Awards ceremony, primed to accept more Oscar gold and shoot off his flabby mouth at the expense of the Republican White House, to the unbridled delight of his liberal-slash-gay Hollywood audience. His red-meat speeches seem calculated to make the Hollywood crowd smile—if only their Botox-frozen facial muscles would let them.

Based on the above description, one would think that we at the Republican National Committee are working overtime to take down the man-mountain known as Michael Moore. In point of fact, nothing could be farther from the truth, because the director of *Fahrenheit 9/11* just might be the most valuable fundraising tool at our disposal. Just mention the name "Michael Moore" in a fundraising letter, and watch the GOP dollars come rolling in. Few other names, with the possible exception of Osama bin Laden, Satan, and Hillary Clinton, can work such magic.

Moreover, Michael Moore is extremely useful as a means to taint other members of the Democrat Party, including those who have absolutely nothing to do with him. Example: After Rep. Jack Murtha (D-Penn.) came out against the war in Iraq, White House press spokesperson Scott McClellan accused him of "endorsing the policy positions of Michael Moore and the extreme liberal wing of the Democratic Party." By linking Murtha to Michael Moore, we were able to obscure the fact that Murtha was a decorated Vietnam War veteran and instead make the public think he was in league with a despised cheeseburger-gorging, tuxedo-button-popping neo-Communist jerk.

In short, Michael Moore is so valuable to us Republicans, we don't want to do anything to harm him. In fact, we want him to be around for a long, long time. And quite frankly, that's what has us worried. Moore's egregious eating habits and lack of exercise has us at the RNC deeply concerned. It's not a good sign when a middle-aged man gets winded while lifting an Oscar statuette. And so, we are doing everything in our power to preserve Michael Moore, infiltrating his inner circle with Republican operatives who will hide Twinkies from him and "forget" to drive him to the set, forcing him to get off his capacious ass and walk. Since our covert operations have begun, Moore has lost a grand total of two pounds. It's not much, but it's a start.

DR. FRIST'S LONG-DISTANCE VIDEOTAPE DIAGNOSES OF LEADING DEMOCRATS

Senate majority leader Bill Frist (R-Tenn.) is not only a great political leader but a brilliant doctor as well. In March of 2005, when doctors at Terri Schiavo's bedside claimed that the woman was in a "persistent vegetative state," the amazing Dr. Frist was able to look at a video of Ms. Schiavo and determine, "She certainly responds to visual stimuli." At the Republican National Committee, we were of course impressed with Dr. Frist's ability to make such an accurate diagnosis based on looking at a videotape, and asked ourselves, how could this talent be used to destroy our Democrat opponents? The answer: We asked Dr. Frist to view videotapes of several leading Democrats and offer his expert diagnoses of lurking medical problems that they have been opportunistically hiding from the American people. The following are the shocking results of Dr. Frist's examinations:

SEN. JOHN KERRY (D-MASS.)

Dr. Frist's Diagnosis:
The patient appears to have droopy eyes, which are often an early sign of myasthenia gravis, a disorder in which the muscles of the eye weaken. If the eye muscles weaken further, it could be hard for the patient to keep his eyes open, which would make him unable to perform many tasks, including finding Osama bin Laden.
CONCLUSION: Patient is unfit to be president of the United States.

SEN. JOHN EDWARDS (D-N.C.)

Dr. Frist's Diagnosis:
The patient wears his hair in a full, lush style that appears designed to hide a noticeable swelling in the forehead. The swelling may have been caused by a head injury or other trauma, indicating that the patient may have suffered a severe brain injury as well.
CONCLUSION: Patient is unfit to be president of the United States.

SEN. HILLARY CLINTON (D-N.Y.)

Dr. Frist's Diagnosis:
The patient has thick, swollen ankles which suggest that her blood is not properly circulating throughout her body. If the blood fails to circulate to her brain, patient could become lightheaded or even pass out while negotiating an arms treaty with North Korea or deciding whether or not to invade Iran. **CONCLUSION: Patient is unfit to be president of the United States.**

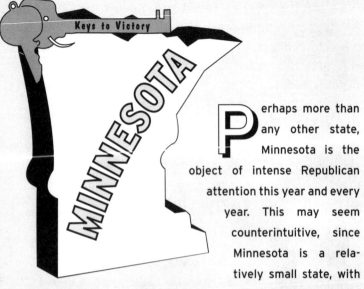

MINNESOTA

Perhaps more than any other state, Minnesota is the object of intense Republican attention this year and every year. This may seem counterintuitive, since Minnesota is a relatively small state, with only ten electoral votes—hardly enough to determine the outcome of a presidential election, especially when we are committing massive voter fraud to guarantee victory in such states as Florida and Ohio. But Minnesota is an important state to us for another reason: It has produced more doomed presidential nominees for the Democrats over the past forty years than any other state except Massachusetts. Therefore, it stands to reason that today's rising stars in Minnesota will someday, a few years hence, be dragging the entire national Democrat Party down to ignominious defeat in November. For this reason and this reason alone, we love Minnesota and call it "The Cradle of Losers."

A quick look at the history books bears out the extremely helpful role that the so-called North Star State has played in delivering the White House, time and time again, to the Republican Party. In 1968, native son Hubert Humphrey lost to Richard M. Nixon, and in 1984, Walter Mondale crashed and burned in his run against President Ronald Reagan, carrying only the District of Columbia and—drum roll, please—Minnesota. This record of futility seems destined to repeat itself yet again as Minnesota is about to play host to the political ambitions of yet another future loser: Al Franken.

That's right: The former *Saturday Night Live* comedian and perennial liberal loudmouth is mulling a Senate run in his home state, and we as Republicans should do everything in our power to ensure that he wins. Why? Simple: A Senator Franken in 2008 will no doubt lead to a presidential nominee Franken in, say, 2016—when Mr. Franken can be counted on to carry the District of Columbia and, just maybe, Minnesota.

How can we best guarantee that Al Franken cruises to an easy Senate win in 2008? Our best bet is to nominate a comedian whom the voters will find even more irritating than him. At this stage of the game, we are still searching for candidates, but so far our short list consists of Andrew Dice Clay, Gallagher, and Carrot Top.

Favorite Comedians:
1) Jeff Foxworthy 2) Larry the Cable Guy 3) Grandpa on "Hee Haw" 4) Screech

DIRTY TRICK: CLAIM THE
DEMOCRATS ARE FRENCH

Of the many things that Americans hate—a list that includes exercising, reading, and waiting—nothing makes our blood boil more than the people, culture, and annoying accent of the French. Our hatred of the French may have reached its apex in 2003 when Jacques Chirac and his Froggy pals refused to join our "Coalition of the Willing" for the invasion of Iraq, preferring to stay at home, sipping lattes and smoking smelly cigarettes in their overpriced cafes. Yes, these Gallic cowards failed to stand by their American allies in a time of need, unlike the brave Kingdom of Tonga, who sent forty troops, or Moldova, who sent twelve.

To exact revenge on these double-dealing frogs, Republicans in the House of Representatives changed the name of "French fries" in the House cafeteria to "freedom fries." While the do-nothing Democrats stood idly by, only the Republicans had the courage to hit the French where it hurts—by changing the name of their celebrated side dish. From that moment on, we have taken every opportunity to link the Democrats with the French in the American people's minds. It's a strategy based on a very simple principle: If people hate the French, just make them think that the Democrats are French and—voila!—they will hate the Democrats, too.

We started to implement this scheme during the 2004 presidential race, when a top White House advisor started a whispering campaign to the effect that John Kerry "looks French." The French label stuck, just showing how powerful one effective ethnic slur, even an entirely bogus one, can be. The looking-French business may have single-handedly cost Kerry the election, even more than our systematic voter fraud in Ohio. And Kerry reinforced the impression that he was French when, on the day after the election, he went on TV and surrendered.

The lesson is clear: When in doubt, make the voters believe that the Democrats are actually Frenchocrats, ready to turn their snooty noses up at any perfectly good war that comes down the pike. Through the clever use of Photoshopping (see below) any Democrat can be made to look French, and this handy Democrat-to-French Conversion Chart can give your favorite Democrat a newly minted French-sounding name.

DEMOCRAT-TO-FRENCH CONVERSION CHART	
Democrat	*French*
Howard Dean	Howard de la Dean
Bill Clinton	Guillaume Clintonne
Joseph Biden	Giscard Boudin
Barbara Boxer	Barbiere Bonaparte
Barack Obama	Jacques Gitano

Through the wonder of Photoshop technology, any Democrat can be made to look instantly French, as in this picture of Sen. Ted de Kennedy.

THE REPUBLICAN ANSWER TO
ROCK THE VOTE: STOP THE VOTE

During the past few elections, the organization known as Rock the Vote has had a simple agenda: get young people engaged in their democracy by encouraging them to register to vote and then express their will at the ballot box. While this goal sounds well-meaning enough, at the Republican National Committee we believe that Rock the Vote's objectives are far more sinister than that. Since the majority of young people tend to vote along single-issue lines that do not square with the Republican agenda—for the legalization of marijuana, say, or the right not to be shot at in Iraq—the lion's share of youngsters registered by Rock the Vote register as Democrats and vote for Democrat candidates. Therefore, to counter the effects of Rock the Vote, the Republican Party has decided to launch its own youth-targeted initiative: Stop the Vote.

Stop the Vote's goals are simple. If Rock the Vote is determined to get young people to vote on election day, Stop the Vote's goal is to get those same young people to do *anything else but vote* on election day. Fortunately, when it comes to being easily distracted, today's generation of weed-smoking iPod-listening slackers are the champs.

The following is just a partial list of ways in which Stop the Vote hopes to encourage young voters that the only party that should have their vote on election day is a keg party!

- On election day, special Stop the Vote vans will fan out across the country and drive up to polling places, where Stop the Vote volunteers will shout through megaphones: "Hey, kids, don't wait in line to vote—they're giving away free Sony PlayStation Portables at Wal-Mart!"

- Rock the Vote has successfully used such MTV stars as Madonna, P. Diddy, and Snoop Dogg to convince young people to vote. Well, look out Democrats, because we Republicans have some rock stars of our own: namely, Ted Nugent and Kid Rock. On election day, the Republican Party will host the largest free rock concert in history, G.O.P.looza™, to make sure that America's youth are rockin' and not votin'. With Ted Nugent and Kid Rock headlining, G.O.P.looza™ promises to be a wholesome blend of music, beer, and unregistered firearms.

- Barb and Jenna Bush will appear on national TV, offering free Jell-O shots to any U.S. citizen under thirty who can prove he did not vote.

Note to self:
Do NOT let
Jenna have keys
to Air Force One

▲
Lesson
3
Disaster Preparedness

Hurricane Katrina and its aftermath proved to be one of the most trying episodes of President George W. Bush's second term. Despite the fact that, as the president's mother pointed out, nature had done the citizens of New Orleans an enormous favor by ridding them of their crappy homes, the government's handling of the disaster turned out to be a public-relations nightmare. Still, the president remained resolute in a time of crisis. "I'm not going to cry about it," he said. "Crying never gets you anywhere, unless you're Anderson Cooper."

In the days following the hurricane, President Bush mulled several options, including hiring a Las Vegas developer to transform the city of New Orleans into a full-size replica of Venice, Italy, complete with gondoliers. After his proposal proved to be too costly, with estimates putting it at "slightly more expensive" than President Reagan's "Star Wars" missile defense system, President Bush chose another option, as the following news clip shows.

Bush Determined to Plan Next Catastrophe

WILL BE 'CATASTROPHIC SUCCESS,' SAYS PRESIDENT

In a nationally televised address last night, President George W. Bush said that Hurricane Katrina had taken him by surprise but promised the American people, "As long as I sit in this chair, all future catastrophes will be planned by me."

Attempting to reassure the country that he had a firm hand on the ship of state, the president said, "If there is going to be a tremendous disaster that impacts thousands or millions of American lives, then it is going to happen on my schedule and on my terms."

Backing up his rhetoric with action, the president said he was going to make disasters a top priority of his administration by creating a cabinet-level post, tentatively called Secretary of Catastrophe.

"It will be the Secretary of Catastrophe's job to devise, plan, and implement all major disasters going forward," the president said.

While Mr. Bush did not indicate whether the next catastrophe would be of an economic, foreign policy, or ecological nature, he concluded with this promise: "The White House will plan the next catastrophe and it will be a catastrophic success."

TURN THE DEMOCRATS
INTO MOMMIES

"**R**epublicans are the Dad party, and Democrats are the Mom party." That mantra, which we at the Republican National Committee repeat dozens of times on a daily basis, has won more elections for Republicans than all the bushels of campaign contributions we've accepted from disgraced lobbyists.

Let's take a moment now and think about what this mantra means. In a family, Mom and Dad perform very different functions. Mom cooks meals, packs lunches for school, and makes sure all of the countertops and furniture in the home are kept shiny and Lemon Pledge fresh. For his part, Dad watches football on TV, drinks beer, and occasionally gets up off the couch to use the bathroom. In this way, both Mom and Dad contribute to a happy home.

But what if a bully moves next door and starts threatening the family with a 12-gauge shotgun? Who do you want to protect the family: Mom, whose expertise is mainly limited to baking and cleaning, or Dad, who is big and strong and has been drinking all day? The answer, of course, is Dad.

You may be asking yourself, what's the point of this story? Quite simply, the United States of America is like a family, and when that family is under attack, it will always turn to Dad. And it is up to us to constantly drum it into voters' heads that we are the Dad—big, strong, and brave—and Democrats are the Mom—little, weak, and cowardly, who sob uncontrollably at the first sign of danger or when we forget their anniversary. In order to coast to victory, our mission is simple: We must turn the Democrats into mommies.

Fortunately, the Democrats make our job easy for us, by constantly associating their party with such "Mom" issues as education, school lunches, and "caring." That leaves us free to grab such core "Dad" issues as national defense, the right to bear arms, and corporal punishment in schools. In essence, we are telling the American people, if you are looking for a party that will invade countries, increase gun ownership, and hit you, we are that party.

Having said that, there's still more that we can do to cement the Democrats' "Mom" role in the voters' psyche. Try this tactic: If you're running for office, spread the rumor that your candidate likes to bake. Start this slowly, and then build, placing hecklers at his rallies waving oven mitts and aprons. In debates, make snide references to his "half-baked" ideas. If the voters are given a choice between a candidate who bakes and one who goes on hunting trips and blows away ducks, on election day it won't even be close.

A FEW WORDS FROM BUSH'S BRAIN

The architect of President George W. Bush's electoral success, political advisor Karl Rove, has often been referred to as "Bush's Brain," except by President Bush himself, whose nickname for Rove is "Turd Blossom." This has caused some at the White House to refer affectionately to Rove as "Bush's Turd." Whether a brain or a turd, one thing is for sure: Karl Rove knows how to win elections like nobody's business. The following are a few choice words of wisdom from this great man.

When I began in politics, the conventional wisdom was, "Attack your opponent's weakness." I tried that for a few years, but it kind of stuck in my craw, because, well, it just didn't seem evil enough to me. I have a pretty good barometer when it comes to political tactics—I call it my "evil-o-meter." And when a tactic seems legitimate and aboveboard and moral, I rip it out of my playbook and come up with something else. In this case, the tactic I devised was, "Attack your opponent's strength." As tactics go, it is very evil, and man oh man does it work!

Let's take the example of John Kerry in 2004. At the Bush campaign, we knew what John Kerry's strength was: He fought in Vietnam and won a Purple Heart for being wounded there. So out came the Swift Boat Veterans for Truth, the stars of countless attack ads who cast doubt on Kerry's bravery and war record. Instead of basking in the glory of his military service, the poor sap had to spend the entire campaign *defending* it. Meanwhile, President Bush remained above the fray, telling reporters, "Take a look at my military record—you won't find anything."

Time and time again, attacking your opponent's strength is the easiest way to take the Democrats down, and here's the beauty part—they never seem to figure it out! Going forward, here is a partial list of Democrat contenders, their strengths, and how to eviscerate them:

SEN. JOSEPH BIDEN (D-DEL.)
Strength: Has represented Delaware in U.S. Senate since 1972
   Attack: Despite his efforts, Delaware remains one of the nation's tiniest states

FORMER GOVERNOR MARK WARNER (D-VA.)
Strength: Young, attractive, appealing to women
Attack: In White House, would be catnip for interns

SEN. HILLARY CLINTON (D-N.Y.)
Strength: Seen as a strong female role model
   Attack: Start whispering campaign that she is a transsexual

True???

ELEPHANTS NEVER FORGET, DONKEYS NEVER REMEMBER

At this point in the *Playbook,* you're probably saying to yourself, "We pull the same sleazy, underhanded tricks on the Democrats year after year—how come they never figure it out?" Or, "Any moron could see our dirty tricks coming from a mile away—how come the Democrats never do?" Or, "How stupid could the Democrats be?" Truth be told, not a day goes by at Republican National Committee headquarters that we don't ask ourselves those questions, or questions like them, many, many times a day. The inability of the Democrats to apply the lessons of one election to the next has been one of the keys to Republican success over the years, right up there with illegal campaign donations and money laundering.

A child will touch a hot stove, get burned, and then never touch it again. A Democrat will touch a hot stove, get burned, and then two years later say, "What's a stove?" Like Charlie Brown to our Lucy, they gladly run at full speed to kick the football, totally forgetting that we have yanked it away at the last second in their previous thousand attempts. Like Wile E. Coyote in the Road Runner cartoons, Democrats suffer the same grindingly repetitive fate every election: falling off cliffs, exploding, and disappearing in a cloud of smoke at the bottom of a canyon. And next election, guess what? They're back for more.

The essential difference between Democrats and Republicans is this: Democrats suffer collective amnesia after each election and revert to their traditional role as patsy in time for the next one, Republicans remember every trick that has worked for them in the past and shamelessly reuse it, regardless of who their Democratic opponent happens to be. How do we get away with it? It's a simple matter of *not repeating the same tactic in two consecutive election years.* The following table shows how to alternate dirty tricks so that the Democrats never figure out that we've used them before. Remember, "Fool me once, shame on you. Fool me twenty times, I'm a Democrat."

ELECTION YEAR ENDING IN	DIRTY TRICK TO FOOL DEMOCRAT WITH
2	Lie about war record
4	Accuse of being a flip-flopper
6	Claim that Social Security is about to crumble
8	Accuse of being weak on defense
0	Say that they burned flag in college

FOREWORD
to the 1988 Edition

By President Ronald Reagan

*P*resident Ronald Reagan was completing his successful *eight-year tenure as president when he wrote the following foreword to the 1988 edition of* The Republican Playbook. *Mr. Reagan credited the* Playbook *with helping him to defeat Democrat incumbent President Jimmy Carter in 1980, since the* Playbook *was the source for his unforgettable "There you go again" zinger that demolished Carter in one of their televised debates. In his foreword, President Reagan shares some of the wisdom he accrued during his eight years in the White House.*

Sometimes people ask me, "President Reagan, what's the most important thing you've done since being elected president of the United States?" They probably expect me to say, negotiated arms control treaties with the Soviet Union, or cut the federal income tax in half, or maybe, invaded Grenada. And while all of those things were accomplishments I'm quite proud of (especially Grenada, which Nancy only told me about recently), none of them is the correct answer. The most important thing I've done since being elected president is clearing brush at my ranch at Santa Barbara.

Now, I can imagine that some of you are scratching your heads right now. You're probably saying, "But President Reagan, clearing brush can't possibly be as important as negotiating an arms treaty with the Soviets—can it?" Well, that's where you're wrong. You see, the minute I start clearing brush at the ranch, pesky reporters can't ask me a bunch of nosy questions, because, well, I'm clearing brush. People naturally assume that I use my time clearing brush to think about things of national importance, like the economy, education, and arms control. The truth is, when I'm clearing brush, I'm thinking about the brush I have to clear.

To tell you the truth, that's why I feel sorry for my Soviet friend, Mikhail Gorbachev. He may be head of an Evil Empire, but he's not a bad egg, and he's under a lot of pressure these days. I'm sure he'd like to get the members of the Politburo off his back, but here's the problem: He can't just go out back of the Kremlin and start clearing brush, because in Moscow they don't have any brush. I have half a mind to send him a shipment of brush seeds he can plant, just as sort of a goodwill gesture. Then I'd make a speech and give my friend Mikhail a good piece of advice: "Mr. Gorbachev, tear down that brush."

Ronald Reagan

RONALD REAGAN

DUELING TIPS FROM ZELL MILLER

Few Democrats have the ability to think like a Republican. Science has borne this out. Recent studies of the brains of Democrats and Republicans have shown that the part of the brain responsible for lying and hatching dirty tricks is well developed in Republican brains, but in the brains of Democrats it is barely the size of a raisin. Given this fact, it is truly remarkable when we come across a Democrat who thinks like one of us, and it makes us wonder if there is something abnormal about his brain. Such a man is former senator Zell Miller of Georgia.

Sen. Miller will be remembered for many things in his storied political career, including his stirring and occasionally terrifying keynote address at the 2004 Republican National Convention. But perhaps the best example of Sen. Miller's gift for "thinking outside the box" was his proposal, while appearing on MSNBC's *Hardball with Chris Matthews,* that dueling be brought back as a vibrant part of American life. A form of conflict resolution that served America well for many years, dueling has wrongly been considered outmoded and barbaric, Sen. Miller believes. In three easy-to-follow steps, Sen. Miller shows how the grand tradition of dueling can serve today's Republican politician:

Step 1:
After liberal journalist starts getting fresh with his questions, throw down your gauntlet and challenge him to a duel.

Step 2:
Before he has a chance to react, brandish your weapon.

Step 3:
Run him through.

Other option:
Have Mr. Cheney
take Chris
Matthews on
hunting trip.

DIVERSITY, AND HOW TO PRETEND WE HAVE IT

One of the most persistent criticisms of the Republican Party is that we only represent a narrow sector of the American people, as opposed to the Democrats, the self-styled party of "diversity." Nothing could be further from the truth, because when it comes to diversity, nobody does it better than the GOP. We are the party of middle-class white males and upper-middle-class white males, tall white males and short white males, skinny white males and morbidly obese white males. We could go on, but we believe that we've amply made our point.

Even though our party is the paragon of diversity, we still get criticized by those whose definition of diversity means including women, minorities, and those who make under $500,000 a year. If that's what is meant by diversity, then it's possible the Republican Party is a wee bit less than diverse, which brings us to the subject of this chapter: If you don't have diversity, pretend to have it. And the best time to do that is every four years at our national nominating convention.

In the olden days, the Republican National Convention served the purpose of choosing the party's nominees for president and vice president. Since those decisions are now made far in advance of the summer gathering, during a multibillion-dollar negative-ad war known as the Iowa Caucuses, the Republican National Convention now has another purpose entirely:

to trick the American people into believing that women and minorities play a large role in the Republican Party.

Truth be told, there are some women and minorities in the upper echelons of the party. Secretary of State Condoleezza Rice, Supreme Court Justice Clarence Thomas, and former secretary of state Colin Powell are three prominent Republican African Americans, although Powell will continue to get less prominent by the day if he doesn't shut his piehole. And Attorney General Alberto Gonzales, a Hispanic, is one of the administration's leading advocates of torture. You don't get more Republican than that.

Still, that's only four people, and in a huge convention hall, those four faces can easily get lost in a sea of white ones. That's why when we put together our roster of convention entertainers, we always hire African American gospel choirs and R & B acts instead of musicians we actually like, like Lee Greenwood. Putting up with music we can't stand once every four years is a small price to pay for maintaining our hammerlock on the White House.

REPUBLICAN MORPH-O-MATIC

Nothing takes down a political opponent like negative ads, and nothing adds sizzle to negative ads like the technique known as "morphing": taking a photograph of your Democrat opponent and gradually turning his or her face into someone

John Kerry
morphs into . . .

Hillary Clinton
morphs into . . .

Howard Dean
morphs into . . .

Joseph Biden
morphs into . . .

else. The great thing about morphing is that unlike other forms of political persuasion, it doesn't require any facts to back it up! Take a look at how morphing can alter the perception of several leading Democrats in the voters' minds

Osama bin Laden

Kim Jong Il

Saddam Hussein

Satan

†ALKING POINTS
Domestic Spying

When President Bush acknowledged that he had conducted wire-tapping without warrants, the outrage from the liberal media was predictable. Pundits and op-ed columnists lashed out at the president's domestic-spying program for a whole host of ridiculous reasons, including the fact that it was against the law. Here at the Republican National Committee we thought to ourselves, if we're going to get our panties in a twist every time we "break the law," we might as well pack it in right now.

The outrage just kept flowing, including charges that wiretapping without warrants was "Nixonian." We're sure that President Bush thought the very same thing we thought: "Thanks for the compliment!"

"Legal" or not, domestic spying is an important tool in the war on terror. This election cycle, the Democrats are sure to try to use it against us, accusing us of Orwellian excesses and that old chestnut: "trampling on the Bill of Rights." Since they intend to make domestic spying a hot-button election issue, it becomes even more important that we develop talking points to confuse the voters about it.

- Let's say you're on the bus, talking on your cell phone, and the person sitting next to you happens to overhear your conversation. Nothing illegal about that, right? Now let's say that the person sitting next to you just happened to be an agent for the NSA. Still legal, right? So the only difference between that scenario and domestic spying is that instead of sitting next to you on the bus, the NSA agent is listening in on your conversation from the comfort of NSA headquarters in Washington, D.C.

- Terrorists talk on their cell phones constantly, thanks to a discount calling plan established by Osama bin Laden called Friends and Terrrrorists™. Under this plan, each al Qaeda member gets up to one thousand minutes a month free if he calls members of his own terror cell.

- By establishing freedom of speech in the Bill of Rights, the framers of the Constitution implicitly established freedom of hearing, meaning that you have the right to say anything you want, but the government has the right to eavesdrop on everything you say. Look it up!

Note to self: Remember to read transcript of Bill Clinton's conversations with phone sex gal.

THE FOX NEWS CHANNEL—
NEWS WE CAN USE

A wholly owned subsidiary of the Republican National Committee, the FOX News Channel has been an effective tool in the election campaigns of Republican candidates. Since its inception in 1996, the "Fair and Balanced" network has become the ratings leader among the all-news networks while providing the public with a reliable, steady stream of fresh-out-of-the-oven Republican propaganda.

In the early days of the FOX News Channel, there were technical glitches that often delayed the transmission of propaganda from Republican officeholders and candidates to the FOX News broadcast headquarters in New York City. Republican politicians were sometimes frustrated as their slanted anti-Democrat rants, beamed by satellite from their offices in Washington, became garbled on their way to the FNC headquarters, and did not make their way into the anchors' mouths for minutes, sometimes hours. To eliminate this problem, we have now developed a new automated system that will enable you to get your words into the FOX anchors' mouths in a matter of seconds:

Idea: take control of weather channel so next hurricane won't look so bad (legal?)

Step 1:
Dial toll-free number that connects you to the FOX News Republican Speedline ™.

Step 2:
Key in your access code.

Step 3:
Speaking slowly, say the opinion you would like a FOX anchor to repeat as news on the air.

Step 4:
The opinion appears in the teleprompter at FOX News studios in New York.

Step 5:
Anchor reads opinion on the air as if it were fact.

REPUBLICAN FIRST LADIES:
DOS AND DON'TS

Traditionally, Republican First Ladies have enjoyed consistently higher approval ratings than their husbands. The reason for this track record of success is clear: While Republican presidents invade countries, accept illegal campaign contributions, and wiretap American citizens, their wives do none of those things. In fact, the ideal Republican First Lady, Laura Bush, is so devoid of personality that some have even wondered if she might be heavily medicated. The truth is, she is not. Being devoid of personality is something Laura Bush has worked very hard to achieve, and she keeps working at it, day in, day out.

If you think being personality-free and Stepford-like is easy, you're wrong. Case in point: former Democrat First Lady Hillary Rodham Clinton. Within weeks of her husband taking office in 1993, when most Republican First Ladies would be busying themselves by spending taxpayers' money on new flatware, what did Ms. Clinton do? Put together a multibillion-dollar proposal for overhauling the nation's health care system. Her approval ratings plummeted, as the American people were repelled by the spectacle of a First Lady attempting to do something productive.

In a sense, Hillary Clinton couldn't help herself. She was a successful lawyer before she became First Lady, and she saw her time in the White House as an extension of a vibrant, active career. This is why it is very important for all prospective

Republican First Ladies not to have a career in the first place. It's only going to make it harder to downshift into inactivity and sloth once your husband gets elected. Once again, the example of Laura Bush is instructive. True, she did have a career before her husband was elected: She was a librarian. However, as careers go, Mrs. Bush's work as a librarian was especially easy to abandon once she got to the White House, largely because her husband owns no books.

Nancy Reagan was one of our most popular Republican First Ladies. What was the secret to her success? Quite simply, the public believed that she made the best use of her time in the White House, consulting with astrologers and psychics to help President Ronald Reagan make effective executive decisions. There's a lesson in this: The American people will always feel more comfortable with a First Lady who is spending all of her time watching the movements of the planets than with one who is trying to secure affordable health care for all.

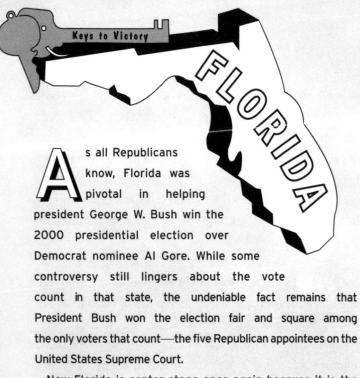

Keys to Victory

FLORIDA

As all Republicans know, Florida was pivotal in helping president George W. Bush win the 2000 presidential election over Democrat nominee Al Gore. While some controversy still lingers about the vote count in that state, the undeniable fact remains that President Bush won the election fair and square among the only voters that count—the five Republican appointees on the United States Supreme Court.

Now Florida is center stage once again because it is the launching pad for the national electoral ambitions of the president's brother, Gov. Jeb Bush. Governor Bush has repeatedly shown that he has "the right stuff" to be president, in spite of being burdened with a first name that makes him sound like a chowderhead. And his brother the president has been a big help to his cause: By increasing the pace of global warming, he has helped create the catastrophic weather conditions that have enabled Gov. Bush to prove his mettle.

Despite his stellar record in the statehouse, Gov. Bush got roughed up in the press for his handling of the Terri Schiavo case, when he attempted to prolong the life of a woman who so-called medical experts said was in a persistent vegetative state. While some Democrats accused the governor of intervening in a situation that was none of his business, the governor knew better. It is always a Republican's job to intervene in situations that are none of his business if it will help him pander to his evangelical Christian base.

The fact is, if Gov. Bush can be faulted for anything, it's for not interfering enough in the Schiavo case. At one point, the governor considered adopting Ms. Schiavo so that he could have control over all of her end-of-life options, but thought better of it. He now realizes what a mistake that was, since it would have increased his campaign contributions from the Christian Right to the tune of one million percent. To correct that error, this year Gov. Bush will offer to adopt all Floridians so that he will have the power to decide when they live and when they die. It's a bold move, and yet another chance to prove that he has what it takes to be president.

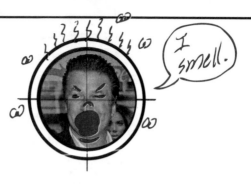

Target:
ALEC BALDWIN

Who is the most annoying Hollywood celebrity Democrat you can think of? Barbra Streisand? Very irritating, but far from the worst. Sean Penn? You're getting warmer. Susan Sarandon? Annoying as all get-out, but since she and Tim Robbins supported Ralph Nader in 2000 and therefore helped elect George W. Bush, we really owe her a debt of thanks and shouldn't be including her on the annoying list at all.

Give up? Okay, we'll tell you. The most annoying Hollywood celebrity Democrat, by far, is Alec Baldwin.

Known as "The Bloviator" for his frequent and tiresome anti-Republican tirades, Alec Baldwin never seems to know when to shut his piehole (especially when there's a second helping of pie available, based on the looks of him). While fewer and fewer Americans seem to attend his movies (*The Cat in the Hat,* anyone?), Mr. Baldwin never misses a chance to use his erstwhile celebrity status to attack the Republican White House. Well, the star of 2001's *The Devil &*

Daniel Webster (didn't see that one, either, huh?) is in for the surprise of his life, because this year the Republican National Committee has decided to target Alec Baldwin.

How will we take down the Bloviator? We have a secret plan to do it, and it goes something like this: Fight Baldwin with Baldwin. The fact is, there's another Baldwin out there, and he's a card-carrying Republican: Adam Baldwin. On the theory that this country is not big enough for two politically active Baldwins, our strategy is to raise the profile and reputation of Adam Baldwin, at the expense of Alec:

◎ Pay off *Inside the Actors Studio* host/pompous ass James Lipton to devote an episode of his show to the oeuvre of Adam Baldwin, where the sycophantic Mr. Lipton will wax rhapsodic about his work on *Stargate SG-1*.

◎ Organize a televised debate between Alec Baldwin and Adam Baldwin. The television cameras, which notoriously add twenty pounds to anyone who appears on TV, will make the buff Adam Baldwin look sinewy and lean, while the Bloviator will appear puffy and blimp-like. Viewers can decide for themselves who has been spending his time studying the issues and who's been parked at the drive-thru window at McDonald's.

◎ Capitalize on sibling rivalry between Baldwin brothers and convince Billy Baldwin to pronounce non-brother Adam Baldwin the victor in the debate with brother Alec Baldwin. A humiliated Alec Baldwin will slouch into obscurity, packing on the pounds as he goes.

▲

Lesson

4

Guantánamo

One of the greatest accomplishments of President George W. Bush's tenure in office has been the establishment of the federal detention center in Guantánamo, Cuba. At Camp X-Ray, terror suspects are held indefinitely in state-of-the-art terror-suspect pens, far, far away from those snoopy pests at Amnesty International. While the president suffered some temporary loss of prestige after *New Yorker* reporter Seymour Hersh uncovered embarrassing photos at the Abu Ghraib prison in Iraq, he put that hard lesson to valuable use: He banned the use of cameras in Guantánamo, and he ordered the wiretapping and twenty-four-hour surveillance of Seymour Hersh.

Despite taking such constructive measures, the president continues to come under fire from critics of so-called "humanitarian abuses" at Guantánamo. The following news clip demonstrates just how deftly President Bush handles the vicious attacks of such critics:

Bush Considers Closing Guantánamo on Wednesdays

PRESIDENT'S PROPOSAL FALLS SHORT OF GITMO OPPONENTS' DEMANDS

Hoping to appease those who have called in recent days for the U.S. to close the detention center at Guantánamo, Cuba, President Bush announced today that he was considering closing the facility on Wednesdays.

Mr. Bush made the proposal in remarks in the White House Rose Garden today, telling reporters, "Under my plan, there would be zero tolerance for abuse of prisoners in Guantánamo, on Wednesdays at least."

Moments after the president made his announcement, opponents of the Guantánamo facility blasted the plan, arguing that closing the detention center one day a week but leaving it open the other six fell far short of the drastic action that was needed.

Sen. Joseph Biden (D-Del.) told reporters, "Guantánamo is a public relations nightmare, and closing it on hump day won't get it done."

Perhaps bowing to such pressure, the president revised his earlier statement, telling reporters that, in addition to Wednesdays, he would be willing to close the facility early on Fridays so that guards could "get a head start on the weekend."

President Jimmy Carter, one of many current and former world leaders who support closing the Guantánamo facility entirely, said that merely closing the detention center on Wednesdays and at noon on Fridays would send the "wrong message" to the Muslim world.

Moments after Mr. Carter made his statement, Mr. Bush offered his official response: "Okay, we'll close it Mondays, Wednesdays, and Fridays but that's my final offer.

FOREWORD
to the 1990 Edition

By President George H. W. Bush

President George H. W. Bush was enjoying his second year in office when he wrote the following foreword to the 1990 edition of The Republican Playbook. *Not the most colorful Republican president in history, President Bush used the foreword to make a spirited defense of his lack of vision. While some of his thoughts about his presidency have, over time, proven somewhat less than prophetic, the foreword is included here to cast light on a man whom history might otherwise forget.*

As I sit here in Kennebunkport having Bloodies with Barbara and the kids, I thought it might be a good time to jot down a few thoughts about being president, especially something that's been a real bee in my bonnet: this whole vision thing.

For the past few months, I've been pounded in the press for not having the vision thing, and I've got to tell you, it is getting pretty darned annoying. I've got news for those reporters out there—having the vision thing is not as important as they think it is. Do they really think I care if I have the vision thing or if I don't have the vision thing? Message: I don't care.

The fact is, you can have the vision thing in spades and still not be an effective politician. Let's take the keynote speaker at the 1988 Democratic National Convention, the governor of Arkansas, Bill Clinton. Now, he seemed like a nice enough fellow over there, but I want to tell you, if ever someone had too much of the vision thing it's that guy. He went on for about half an hour, and I've got to tell you, there's a fine line between having the vision thing and having diarrhea of the mouth. Again, he seems like an intelligent enough young man, but mark my words, his political career is over.

If I had to pick one man of the next generation who does have the vision thing, but who also knows when to shut his trap, it's the fine young man I chose as my running mate, Vice President Dan Quayle. If I were a betting man, I'd say that after I'm through serving eight years in office, the American people will rally around Dan as their next president for another eight years. And someday, in the heat of a presidential debate, a Republican candidate will be able to say, "I knew Dan Quayle. Dan Quayle was a friend of mine. Senator, you're no Dan Quayle."

George Bush

GEORGE H.W. BUSH

HOW TO DRAIN ALL SPONTANEITY FROM YOUR TOWN HALL MEETINGS

Increasingly popular in recent years, so-called town hall meetings are an opportunity for political candidates and officeholders to meet face-to-face with their constituents in a free, open exchange of ideas. Unlike rallies or other staged political events, the town hall is an unstructured, unrehearsed forum that enables ordinary people to ask tough questions of politicians, often throwing them a curveball or "getting up in their grille" when they least expect it. A free-for-all in which anything can happen and often does, a town hall meeting is democracy at its best.

NOT! If the description above describes a town hall meeting that you as a Republican politician have ever been subjected to, fire your crappy advance team at once and get some actual professionals working for you. The entire goal of a town hall meeting is to give the appearance of spontaneity while making sure that spontaneity has been totally eliminated from the event, down to the tiniest detail. This means distributing questions written by your staff on three-by-five cards to selected audience members in advance, but more importantly, it means weeding out of the crowd anyone who might heckle or harass you, or ask you something tricky. To assemble the perfect audience for a successful town hall meeting, please use the Republican Town Hall Audience Questionnaire (*opposite*):

Republican Town Hall Audience Questionnaire

1) I would describe myself as a

   a) Republican
   b) Democrat
   c) Independent

NOTE: If you did not answer "a," you do not have to fill out the rest of the questionnaire. Thank you for your time.

2) In the past six months, I have

   a) lost my job
   b) lost my health insurance
   c) made a killing in the stock market thanks to the cut in capital gains taxes

3) I think the country is

   a) moving in the right direction
   b) moving in a fantastic direction
   c) perfect

4) I think Hillary Clinton is

   a) an impressive woman
   b) a well-respected senator
   c) Satan's evil spawn

5) When I am given a three-by-five card to read on television, I

   a) read it over to make sure I agree with it
   b) refuse to read it if it does not represent my opinion
   c) read it verbatim like a robot

SCAPEGOATS 2006:
AN ELECTION-YEAR GUIDE

Webster's Dictionary defines "scapegoat" as "a goat upon whose head are symbolically placed the sins of the people after which he is sent into the wilderness in the biblical ceremony for Yom Kippur," with additional definitions, including "one that bears the blame for others" and "one that is the object of irrational hostility." Here at the Republican National Committee we have another definition of "scapegoat": "a person or persons for us to dump on relentlessly between now and election day, guaranteeing an easy victory at the polls over the Democrats, who are too stupid or lazy to come up with a decent scapegoat themselves."

Choosing an effective scapegoat is easier said than done. The primary criteria for picking a scapegoat are as follows: The scapegoat must be someone whom everybody hates already, someone who has no intention of supporting the Republican Party anyway or, best of all, someone who is totally defenseless and may not even have the right to vote.

Using the supercomputer at the Republican Party's sister organization, the Federal Bureau of Investigation, we were able to sift through thousands and even millions of leading candidates for scapegoats for the 2006 fall campaign, and in a matter of 4.6 seconds came up with the following winners:

- **IMMIGRANTS:** They don't look like us, they don't talk like us, and they are taking our jobs. What's there to like about immigrants? Nothing. Correction: One thing to like about immigrants is that they make fabulous scapegoats, and here's the beauty part—the illegal ones can't vote! Let's use Election 2006 to put America's undocumented workers in their place, and after the election, they can go back to toiling in the homes and gardens of Republican officeholders.

- **HOLLYWOOD:** Increasingly, we live in a society plagued by gun violence and teenage sex. Is it too pat and simplistic to blame all of these woes on Hollywood? One rule of thumb at the RNC is that if blaming someone seems too pat and simplistic, go for it! By scapegoating Hollywood we run practically no risk of losing votes among the Tinseltown crowd, since almost all of them are Democrats anyway, except for Clint Eastwood, Charlton Heston, and the guy who played Gopher on *The Love Boat*.

- **THE HOMELESS:** Lying in the middle of the street, begging for money, thrusting their cardboard signs in our faces—any way you slice it, the homeless make it harder for us to get to work in the morning, throwing a monkey wrench in the well-oiled engine of American capitalism. As Republicans, our core constituency is "the second homeless," voters who are earning over $250,000 a year but have still not been able to buy a second home. As for the homeless, it's time to send them a clear, simple message: "Homeless, Go Home."

OFFICIAL REPUBLICAN
SLOGAN GENERATOR

A good slogan can make or break a political campaign. Unlike domestic programs, which aim to solve problems like illiteracy and poverty, or a coherent foreign policy, whose goal is to improve our national security and standing in the international community, slogans serve no purpose whatsoever but to win votes. And here's the best part: Slogans cost nothing at all. As the saying goes, "Talk is cheap," and no one has produced more cheap talk over the years than Republicans.

In order to be successful, a political slogan must be short and catchy, but more importantly, it must sound like it means something while meaning practically nothing at all. "No Child Left Behind" is a great example of that. At first glance, it's hard to disagree with a slogan like that; after all, who is in favor of leaving children behind? Leaving children behind is a very mean thing to do. But what does the slogan mean? You can think about it all the livelong day if you want, but you still won't come up with an answer. It means nothing, which is why it is so excellent.

A bad slogan, on the other hand, is one that means too much. If a slogan seems to set forth a specific policy goal, it is a disaster and should be discarded at once. For example, "Invading Countries That Have a Lot of Oil," while a noble agenda, is a great example of a slogan that should be avoided. A better slogan for that same policy would be "Keeping Nations Free."

Over the past decade, we at the Republican National Committee have developed the Official Republican Slogan Generator (see below). Take one word from column A, add it to a word from column B, and finish with a word from column C, and you're in business!

A	B	C
Keeping	Americans	Here
Making	Workers	Work
Leaving	Babies	Alone
Giving	Jobs	Away
Helping	Pets	Survive
Keeping	Children	Accountable
Making	Evildoers	Dead

TALKING POINTS
Gay Westerns

Of all the threats being posed to American life in the twenty-first century—environmentalism and civil libertarianism, to name just two—perhaps none is as virulent and potentially destructive to our way of life as the threat posed by gay westerns. If films like *Brokeback Mountain* are permitted to sashay into the mainstream of American life, it is only a matter of time before other traditionally heterosexual forms of entertainment, like NASCAR, motocross, and monster truck rallies, become gay as well. It is up to us as Republicans to nip this process in the bud, and that is why, this election cycle, we are proposing a constitutional amendment to ban gay westerns.

Of course, taking such a position could leave us open to charges that the Republican Party is homophobic. That is why it will be increasingly important to stick to the following talking points as the national debate over gay westerns heats up:

- If gay westerns are permitted to proliferate, there will be a disastrous political consequence, as liberal legislatures in several Western states will attempt to legalize marriage between gay cowboys. Should this development concern the average American taxpayer? Absolutely. As gay cowboys wed, they will naturally demand medical and dental benefits, sending the American economy into a tailspin from which it will never recover.

- The rise of gay westerns could lead to a rise in gay country music, which is almost too upsetting to think about. Songs like "Mama, Don't Let Your Sons Grow Up to Be Homosexual Cowboys" could be performed on the stage of the Gay Ole Opry if we don't take action now.

- The cowboy is only one gay icon featured in the 1970s disco band the Village People. That means if gay cowboy movies are allowed to be produced, we may soon see movies featuring gay Indians, gay construction workers, gay cops, and gay bikers. How do you bring about the end of American society? As a certain senator might say, "It takes a Village Person."

WHEN IN DOUBT, CUT TAXES

Every now and then, in the middle of a political race, a Republican actually finds himself behind a Democrat in the polls. This is a mystifying state of affairs, especially if the Republican candidate has been following all of the advice in this *Playbook* and has lied about the Democrat's war record, suggested that his wife is a lesbian, or Photoshopped pictures of him grabbing Jane Fonda's ass. Still, in some very rare cases, all of these foolproof tactics are not sufficient to get the job done. At moments like these, it's time to bring out the heavy guns: Promise the voters that you will cut taxes.

As Republicans, we have learned to worship the tax cut as the all-purpose political panacea. It's not hard to see why. People hate taxes, and so it makes sense that if you promise to eliminate taxes, they will love you. If Republicans could find a way to eliminate other things that people hate, like death or Paris Hilton, we would promise that, too.

For some reason, Democrats have stubbornly refused to go along with the premise that tax cuts always work. That's good news for us, because that paints them into a corner where they actually appear to *support* the idea of taxes. Case in point: At the 1984 Democratic National Convention, Democrat nominee Walter Mondale said, "Let's tell the truth. Mr. Reagan will raise taxes, and so will I. He won't tell you. I just did." At the Republican National Committee headquarters, we heard those words

and burst into spontaneous tears of gratitude. Sometimes the Democrats make our job a little too easy.

By warning the voters that our tax cuts will be ruinous to the economy, the Democrats invariably cast themselves as the "tax and spend" party, as opposed to us Republicans, who are merely the "spend" party. This is a huge political advantage for us, because voters love to spend, but hate being taxed. An example: Go to a Circuit City store at the height of Christmas season, and see the people buying portable DVD players, Sony PlayStations, and gigantic plasma screens. See how happy they are? Now contrast that with people in an H&R Block office as April 15 approaches. Not too many smiles there, are there? Lesson learned: spending good, taxes bad.

During an election campaign, don't be surprised if your Democrat adversary puts your feet to the fire and asks you how you intend to pay for our party's huge military spending programs, Homeland Security budget, etc., if you are cutting taxes. You already have a surefire answer up your sleeve: "More tax cuts."

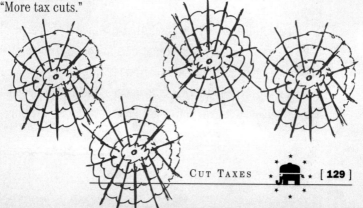

THE POLITICS OF
PERSONAL DESTRUCTION:
A BEGINNER'S GUIDE

During that giddy and glorious time known as the impeach-ment of Bill Clinton, barely a day went by that the Clintons or their surrogates didn't proclaim to the press, "The politics of personal destruction must stop." At the Republican National Committee, we had this response: "Why? It sure is working!" On this issue as on so many others, the Democrats are wrong and we are right.

The "politics of personal destruction"—the art of winning an election by ruining the other candidate's reputation and, if you're doing it right, career—gets a bad rap. The Democrats claim that it's dirty pool, and that it demeans our democracy and turns off the voters. We beg to differ. If you flicked on the TV one afternoon and had a choice between watching a meeting of the Ways and Means Committee on C-SPAN, or a salacious report about a senator's affair with a tranny hooker, which would you pick? Far from being a turnoff, the politics of personal destruction stokes the embers of our democracy and keeps it ablaze.

Some political beginners think that the politics of personal destruction is a simple matter of dredging up some unfounded allegations, putting them out there, and letting them work their magic. If only it were that easy. Remember, the goal of the politics of personal destruction is not merely to defeat the opponent, but *to ruin the rest of his or her life.* In order to accomplish this, make sure you have done everything on the following politics of personal destruction checklist:

- **BE BOLD.** Some novices try to bring down an opponent by making allegations about things they actually did. Mistake! No one ever lost an election because of jaywalking or overdue library books. If you're not accusing your opponent of selling crystal meth to welfare mothers or trafficking in Thai sex slaves, you're just not trying.

- **REPEAT YOUR ALLEGATIONS RELENTLESSLY.** Once you make your allegations, stick with them, restating them over and over again. This is a tactic endorsed by every great political strategist, from Joseph Goebbels to Karl Rove.

- **NEVER ADMIT YOU ARE WRONG.** Even if your opponent produces unshakable evidence that you have been fibbing about him, under no circumstances should you admit that you have been mistaken. Remember, there will be plenty of time to apologize—after the election.

TALKING POINTS

The Environment

You can count on the Democrats to tout themselves to the voters as the environmentalist party. Every election year, they hold themselves up as the protectors of the ecology, and paint the Republicans as rapacious probusiness villains who will not rest until the earth is literally scorched. The Democrats are not alone in tarring us in this way. Their pals at the Sierra Club and the World Wildlife Fund, and even those bird-loving lunatics at the Audubon Society, enjoy making us look like we get our jollies by kicking Mother Nature in the fanny.

Yes, there is no shortage of groups who claim to protect the environment. At the Republican National Committee, however, we'd like to change the terms of the debate, and ask: Does the environment need protecting? Turn on the Weather Channel. Every two days, it seems, a hurricane or tsunami is pounding a city, causing untold casualties and billions in property damage. Any thinking person would have to come to the same conclusion that we at the RNC have: Rather than protect the environment, we should be protecting ourselves from the environment.

Of course, even though this is the only logical stance to take on this subject, our plan to make the environment the enemy in the upcoming election will be unpopular in some states, especially those that have lots of trees and cute animals. That is why we must pound away relentlessly at the following talking points:

■ Those who oppose the drilling in the Arctic National Wildlife Refuge say that oil exploration in the Arctic wilderness will endanger wildlife there, such as the polar bear. Show voters pictures of people who have been mauled by bears and ask, do these furry evildoers really need our help?

■ In states like Massachusetts that have legalized gay marriage, it's worth asking: Where are we going to get the oil necessary to fuel all of those limousines that the bridegrooms will ride off to their honeymoons in? The Arctic National Wildlife Refuge, that's where.

■ Critics of the administration's environmental policies say that they have led to more catastrophic weather conditions, like hurricanes. But thanks to hurricanes, Nielsen ratings and ad revenues at the leading cable news networks are at record high levels. Take that, doomsayers!

Proposed change in Tax Code— claim countries you've invaded as dependents

Keys to Victory

NEW YORK

Much as we at the Republican National Committee would like them to, Bill and Hillary Clinton just won't go away. When Bill Clinton left office, we were pretty sure that he would leave public life, open his presidential library in Little Rock, and then spend most of his time chasing tube tops at Hooters. No such luck. He has continued to be a vocal critic of the White House, and to make matters worse, has actually raised his public profile by helping victims of Hurricane Katrina, the Asian tsunami, and other weather catastrophes. We didn't used to think there were any downsides to global warming, but Bill Clinton's rising popularity is certainly one of them.

Hillary has been even worse. Elected to the Senate in 2000, she has actually enjoyed tremendous popularity up and down the state and appears poised to coast to an easy win in the upcoming election. This is bad news for us, since it means that she will be even better positioned to make a credible run for the presidency in 2008. (It is, however, good news for Bill Clinton, since it means she will be away on the campaign trail, leaving him free to grab all the tail he wants on the disaster relief circuit.) In short, the challenge for us is clear: We must stop Hillary in New York, before she ever gets to the White House—or, as we call it at RNC headquarters, the Armageddon Scenario.

How will we stop Hillary? Our best bet is to bring out of retirement the hardy band of brothers who brought down John Kerry in 2004: The Swift Boat Veterans for Truth. We have already contacted most of these heroes, and they are raring to see some more action in an all-out attack-ad war against the junior senator from New York. In a series of attack ads currently being filmed in Vice President Dick Cheney's secure undisclosed location buried miles beneath the earth's surface, the Swift Boaters are claiming that Hillary led a self-appointed guerilla campaign during the Vietnam War to sink several Swift boats in the Mekong Delta. We have every reason to believe that the Swift Boat ads will send Hillary on a one-way trip to defeat from which she will never recover. If not, we'll just say that she plans to raise taxes.

HOT DEBATE TIPS

Presidential debates entered the modern era in 1960, when Richard Nixon and John F. Kennedy faced off in the first-ever nationally televised debate. While many who listened to the debate on the radio were convinced that Nixon had won, television viewers reached a different conclusion, largely because Kennedy appeared cool and confident while Nixon perspired profusely. Consequently, ever since that historic contest, the Republican National Committee has bribed the stage manager at each debate venue to train high-wattage lights on the Democrat to make him bake in the heat and sweat like a pig.

While this dirty trick has provided us with a certain tactical advantage, it is often not enough to win a debate. In order to do that, the RNC has selected the following two debate tips which should help a Republican nominee go into battle certain of victory.

- **CHANGE THE SUBJECT BEFORE THE SUBJECT CHANGES YOU.**
  The debate moderators, typically culled from the liberal media elite, are only there to sabotage you, and will predictably ask you questions on subjects that are guaranteed to make you look bad, such as your "record." The only way to deal with these questions is by not answering them, and instead answering questions of your own invention. Example:

Q: Under your presidency, the deficit has risen to record levels. How can you hope to cut the deficit without raising taxes?

A: Jim, that's an interesting question, and one I'd like to answer. But before I do, let me address this whole issue of stem-cell research.

Fortunately, the liberal media hack will be too polite to point out that you didn't answer his question. Loser!

- **USE MOVIE CATCHPHRASES TO MAKE YOUR POINT.** Very few Americans like politics, but who doesn't love a good movie? If you really don't have anything of substance to say, just use a quote from a movie instead. Example: Whenever a moderator asked candidate Arnold Schwarzenegger about anything, he always responded, "I will be the Terminator," to guaranteed applause. Try it yourself: When your Democrat opponent proposes an expensive domestic program, say "Show me the money!" Catchphrase to avoid: "I wish I knew how to quit you."

THE BEAUTY OF A
WELL-TIMED LEAK

One of a Republican president's most sacred obligations is to communicate directly with the American people, and there is no better way for him to do that than by using anonymous subordinates to leak information to the press. The ability to plant leaks and subsequently to deny planting them can make the difference between a successful presidency and a failed one. By the yardstick of leaks per day in office, the presidency of George W. Bush must rank as one of the most successful in American history.

Of course, the practice of leaking has its critics, predictable enough, among the liberal media elite. Case in point: The Bush administration has been raked over the coals for leaking the identity of a CIA agent, Valerie Plame. And yet, the uproar over this incident is illogical, at best. Valerie Plame was a secret agent, so it was her job to make sure that her identity remained a secret, not the White House's.

Leaking, and subsequently denying that you did the leaking, is a dark and mysterious science that takes years to master. The following news clipping (*opposite*) shows how the White House has mastered this art in a way that is second to none.

Unnamed White House Source Denies Leak

White House Denies Leaking Denial

An unnamed White House source last night vigorously denied leaking classified information about a CIA operative, sending the White House scrambling to identify the source of the leaked denial.

The unnamed source, who identified himself only as "Rarl Kove," leaked a strongly worded denial of the previous leak in phone conversations with over two hundred newspaper columnists across the country.

"We are not in the business of leaking information," the unnamed source said.

Ben Trimble, a political columnist for the Canton (OH) *Star-Ledger,* attempted to STAR-69 the call in order to identify the source of the leaked denial, but to no avail.

"It wouldn't disclose the phone number or the location," Mr. Trimble said. "That kind of made me think it was Cheney."

White House spokesman Scott McClellan said that the administration would launch a "full investigation" into the leak denials.

"If someone is out there denying leaks, that is very serious business," Mr. McClellan said. "Denying leaks is my job."

But moments after Mr. McClellan spoke, columnists received a new round of anonymous phone calls, this time denying that the White House had been the source of the earlier denials.

As the number of anonymous leaks from the White House mounts to a dozen or more a day, newspaper columnists are increasingly signing up for the federal "do not call" list to keep unnamed White House sources from bothering them at home.

"The first couple of leaks I didn't mind," said the *Star-Ledger*'s Trimble. "But these guys keep calling me at dinnertime."

Keys to Victory

TEXAS

"Don't mess with Texas," President George W. Bush has been known to say, but those sage words of advice haven't kept those pesky Democrats from trying to mess with the president's home state. Do the Democrats actually have designs on Texas? They have about as much shot at carrying the Lone Star State as Dick Cheney has of being named Entertainer of the Year at the Soul Train Music Awards. No, the Democrats have something else in mind entirely. They would like to embarrass the president in Texas, hoping that his national prestige will suffer. Well, if the Democrats intend to mess with Texas, we intend to mess with them, and we are much better at creating a mess than they are.

The Democrats' campaign of harassing the president in his home state started in 2004, with the totally unjustified indictments of the top executives at Enron, one of the most innovative and well-run corporations in the country, second only to Halliburton. The Democrats still hope to link the president to former Enron CEO Ken Lay on the thin shred of evidence that the president once called him "Kenny Boy." This argument is flimsy at best, since it totally ignores the fact that the president has nicknames for everyone; in fact, he calls North Korean dictator Kim Jong Il "Kimmy Boy."

Step two in the Democrats' plan came in the summer of 2005, when they planted antiwar protester Cindy Sheehan outside the president's ranch in Crawford, Texas. The liberal media provided the daily drumbeat of outrage, trying to coax the president into a face-to-face meeting with the publicity-hungry Ms. Sheehan. But the president remained resolute, hiding in his ranch house until she went away.

No doubt, the Democrats will try to use the indictment of former House majority leader Tom DeLay to deliver the fatal blow to the Texas Republican Party, since Rep. DeLay is one of the most formidable fundraisers the state party has ever seen. Well, the joke's on them: If Rep. DeLay winds up in prison, he will be able to continue to raise money from former Enron executives, who will no doubt be just a few cells away. As a wise man once said, "Don't mess with Texas."

▲

Lesson

5
Exit Strategy

A t many junctures of his presidency, George W. Bush has been accused of having no "exit strategy" for U.S. troops in Iraq. In point of fact, just the opposite is true. One exit strategy that has been on the drawing board for months is patterned after the exit strategy of former members of President Bush's cabinet: All of the U.S. troops in Iraq would tender their resignations, saying that they want to spend more time with their families. As simple as this solution is, though, it does bring with it certain complications. As Vice President Cheney so wisely put it at an Oval Office meeting not long ago, "We could bring all the troops home today, but unfortunately, all the oil would still be over there."

Under increasing pressure to announce an exit strategy, President Bush worked overtime to devise one that would satisfy everyone. The following news clip reveals the fruits of those efforts, and offers yet another instructive glimpse into the mind of a master Republican statesman.

BUSH PROMISES TO BRING TROOPS HOME THROUGH IRAN
Most Direct Route, President Says

UNDER PRESSURE to detail an exit strategy for Iraq, President George W. Bush said at a White House briefing today that he would not designate an exact timetable for a withdrawal of U.S. troops but added, "The fastest way to bring the troops home would be through Iran."

After reporters audibly gasped, the president explained that bringing the troops home through Iran would be "the most direct route" and produced driving directions from MapQuest to back up his claim.

But less than an hour after his remarks, Iranian president Mohammad Khatami blasted Mr. Bush's exit strategy, arguing that bringing U.S. troops home through Iran was far from the most direct route, and was, in fact, going totally in the wrong direction.

Using a map of the world and a magic marker, President Khatami showed that by traveling east rather than west, U.S. troops would have to circumnavigate the globe in order to reach their final destination.

In response, Mr. Bush acknowledged that it would be a long journey, but added, "If necessary, we'll stop in North Korea."

DENY KNOWING ANYTHING
ABOUT ANYTHING GOING ON AT
THE WHITE HOUSE

During the height of the 1980 presidential campaign, while American hostages were being held in Iran, some genius at the Democratic National Committee decided that it would be a good idea to produce a campaign ad showing President Jimmy Carter burning the midnight oil, working into the wee hours of the night at the White House. The message these ads were supposed to send was that Carter was a hands-on executive, well versed in all the details of his job, a man who had "done his homework." On election day, Carter was soundly defeated by Ronald Reagan, a man who became famous for watching westerns on TV in the afternoon before dozing off for his daily nap. Is there a lesson to be learned from this? Yes, in a contest between the person who knows what is going on in the White House and one who does not, the person who has no idea what is going on will always win. And that person, invariably, will be the Republican.

History shows us time and time again that if you pit a man who has done his homework against a man who has not, the homework doer will always lose. Take Al Gore versus George Bush in 2000. Gore was the typical brainiac, bragging about having invented the Internet and knowing the name of the president of Russia. President Bush, on the other hand, wore his mediocre college record like a badge of honor. Even though Al

Gore actually won the election and we stole it from him, the fact remains that most Americans did not do their homework in school and do a half-assed job at work, and they relate more to a president who doesn't appear to be breaking a sweat, either.

Not appearing to know what is going on at the White House has served Republican presidents well for decades, especially when a scandal erupted. President Reagan denied knowing anything about Iran-Contra, and the American people believed him, because they assumed the plot was hatched during one of his famous naps. And no one ever linked President Bush to Abu Ghraib, because few Americans believed that he could even pronounce "Abu Ghraib." The fact is, the American people don't want a president who has his hands on the levers of power and is in charge of the country at all times. That's what the Vice President is for.

THE WAR ON TERROR
IS YOUR FRIEND

Before we begin this chapter, let's start with a little quiz. The "war on terror" is:

a) the struggle of Western democracies against Islamic extremism
b) a political ploy to keep Republicans in power
c) both of the above
d) both of the above, but a lot more "b" than "a"

If you answered "d," you are correct. If you answered "b," you are almost correct, and deserve partial credit. "C" is also a pretty good answer. But if for some reason you answered "a," you should probably read this chapter eight or nine times, because your head is definitely up your ass.

Yes, it is true that there are Islamic terrorists in the world. But a war against them would be called the "war on terrorists." The phrase "war on terror," on the other hand, makes no sense at all. You can't declare war on a human emotion. Think about it: If we defeat terror, what's next? Shyness?

While the war on terror doesn't make much sense as a war, it makes a tremendous amount of sense as a political device to advance the Republican agenda and consolidate Republican

power. It's this simple: Whenever you have a program or law you want to propose that seems the least bit shady, all you have to do is invoke the "war on terror." A good example, of course, is the Patriot Act. The Patriot Act is almost as brilliant a name as the "war on terror" because it suggests that anyone who opposes it is not a Patriot. Much like the terrorists themselves, those who oppose the Patriot Act—namely, Democrats and *New York Times* op-ed columnists—must hate our freedom. A convincing way to make this argument would be, "Anyone who says that the Patriot Act tramples on our freedom hates our freedom."

Another good way to exploit the "war on terror" is by the well-timed use of the phrase, "or the terrorists win." Essentially, you should always be prepared to make the case that if the Republican agenda does not become law, the terrorists have somehow won. For example: "If we do not repeal the inheritance tax, then the terrorists win." No one will question the logic of statements like that, unless they want to be accused of hating our freedom.

As you can see, the war on terror is one of the best inventions the Republican Party has ever come up with, right up there with secret CIA torture camps and warrantless wiretaps. You might be asking yourself, what will the party do when the war on terror is over? Answer: The war on terror will be over when we say it's over, and that means never.

ouisiana has been comfortably in the red-state column for years, but the Democrats are sure to try to change that, emboldened by the bad publicity the White House suffered in the aftermath of Hurricane Katrina. Let's get something straight: We at the Republican National Committee know that hurricanes are bad. But there's no disputing the fact that the liberal media, led by professional crybaby Anderson Cooper, blew Katrina completely out of proportion. It was a disaster, yes, but the worst disaster in our nation's history? Aren't we forgetting a little thing called the Lewinsky affair?

Democrats will no doubt try to remind voters in the fall about all of the supposed missteps made by the federal government in the days following Katrina. That's why it's up to us, as Republicans, to start spreading the good news about Katrina. That's right, the good news. There are two sides to every story, even a story about a devastating hurricane that submerged a city in water and left tens of thousands of people homeless. And who better to spread the good news about Katrina than one of the most respected women in America, former First Lady Barbara Bush?

The Republican National Committee has enlisted the former First Lady to crisscross the state between now and the election to tell the pro-Katrina story as only she can. Some of the highlights of her positive message are as follows:

- Former Federal Emergency Management Agency chief Michael Brown got ripped in the press for taking too much time to respond after Hurricane Katrina hit. But if he had responded right away, wouldn't that have made it look like he was alarmed, creating a panic? By taking his time, Michael Brown projected a calm, relaxed air that put the people of New Orleans at ease. If you look at it that way, Brownie did do a heckuva job, and we salute him.

- Thanks to Katrina, New Orleans received worldwide media coverage, something it has not gotten since it hosted the Super Bowl in 2002.

- True, the city was totally submerged in water, but for the first time in years, there were no producers of *Girls Gone Wild* on the streets trying to convince drunken coeds to take off their tops.

OCTOBER SURPRISES:
THE NUCLEAR OPTION

A so-called October Surprise, in which the party in power uses all the advantages of incumbency to create an eleventh-hour international crisis, domestic state of emergency, or full-on war in order to secure victory at the polls in November, is one of the greatest gifts our democracy has to offer. Although Republicans are particularly adept at trumping up October Surprises, the strategy is not unique to the GOP, or even to American politics. Perhaps the most famous October Surprise was manufactured by Soviet premier Nikita Khrushchev, who placed nuclear missiles in Cuba in October of 1962, leading to a tense standoff with U.S. president John F. Kennedy and sending Khrushchev's approval numbers soaring in the Russian polls. Only after a high-ranking member of the Politburo reminded Khrushchev that he was a totalitarian dictator and did not have to worry about running for election in November did the Soviet premier withdraw the missiles from Cuba and go away quietly.

Over the years, Democrats have attempted to engineer October Surprises, but have generally lacked the sneakiness necessary to pull off a real doozy. In the 2004 election, for example, there was some speculation that Democrat nominee John Kerry's wife Teresa Heinz Kerry might hold the world's supply of ketchup, mustard, and other condiments hostage to blackmail the American people into electing her husband. Ultimately, this turned out to be merely a rumor—in fact, a rumor that we started. In the end, John Kerry's only October Surprise was that he was even more boring in October than he was in September, and the rest is history.

If we follow all of the directions in the preceding pages of this mighty *Playbook*, it is unlikely that our party will need to spring an October Surprise on an unsuspecting American public—but you never know. So, just in case, here are four October Surprises that can't help but guarantee us a glorious victory in November:

OCTOBER SURPRISE NUMBER ONE

On the last Sunday in October, President Bush will use the Emergency Broadcast System to interrupt every NFL game being broadcast in America. In a brief but effective address, he will announce that he is releasing all of the Strategic Petroleum Reserve, sending gasoline plummeting to the low, low price of five cents a gallon. Giddy gas-guzzling voters will vote Republican in record numbers, causing a freaked-out Sen. Robert Byrd (D-W.Va.) to switch to the Republican Party after 113 years as a Democrat. On the morning after election day, President Bush will abruptly turn off the spigot, sending gas prices spiking skyward to eight dollars a gallon and oil stocks soaring on Wall Street. In other words, everybody wins.

continues on following page

OCTOBER SURPRISE NUMBER TWO

In a series of top-secret negotiations, the White House agrees to give North Korean madman Kim Jong Il the nuclear reactor he has long hungered for. In exchange, the mercurial Kim agrees to appear in a series of slickly produced campaign ads in which he gives a wholehearted endorsement of Hillary Clinton. The Democrats go down to defeat by a record margin, and the day after the election, we bomb North Korea's nuclear reactor, blowing it to smithereens.

OCTOBER SURPRISE NUMBER THREE

Under cover of darkness, a special ops force digs a big hole in the sand in the Iraqi beach and buries an enormous cache of weapons of mass destruction. The weekend before the election, President Bush makes a surprise trip to Iraq to visit the troops and, on a whim, decides to take a walk on the beach with a metal detector. In no time at all, he "discovers" Saddam's long-lost cache of weapons. Mission accomplished—again!

OCTOBER SURPRISE NUMBER FOUR

On Halloween, Osama bin Laden is finally moved from the basement of the Skull and Bones club at Yale, where he has been held prisoner for the last four years. A military helicopter transports him to Chappaqua, New York, where he is dropped into the backyard of Bill and Hillary Clinton. The Chappaqua Police are tipped off, and they pounce on Bin Laden within minutes. The Clintons are hard-pressed to explain why the world's most wanted man was, even to the most objective observer, their houseguest for the past four years. Both Clintons are tried for treason, ensuring GOP victories for the remainder of the century.

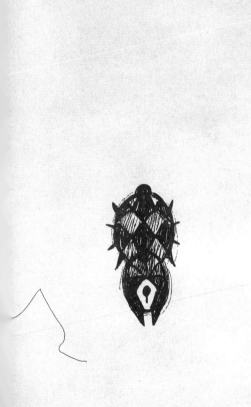

INDEX

CREDITS

Packaged by BTDNYC

    Art Direction and typography: Beth Tondreau

    Research: Scott Ambrosino, Suzanne Dell'Orto

    Art and logo fakesimiles:

        Scott Ambrosino (Elephant FauxLogo throughout and pages 18–19, 23, 25, 27, 36–37, 40–41, 43, 47, 50–51,62–63, 83, 106–107,126–127, 132–133); Scott Ambrosino and Suzanne Dell'Orto (pages 84, 87, 112, 134, 140, 148); Adrian Kitzinger (pages 32–35); Liney Li (pages 11, 13–15); Punyapol "Noom" Kittayarak (pages 31, 75, 91, 104–105, 117, 139, 143); David Sansevere, Jr. (pages 47, 60–61, 69, 101, 109)

        Blue notes and caricatures and doodles throughout: David Sansevere, Jr.

    Typesetting and page layout: BTDNYC

Photo credits:

    Corbis Photo Credits:

    Pages 11, 13-15, 25, 36-37, 57, 83, 87, 105, 125

Page 65

John Kerry testifying before Congress on Vietnam War

http://ice.he.net/~freepnet/kerry/index.php?topic=Testimony

Donald Rumsfeld meeting Saddam Hussein

http://www.gwu.edu/~nsarchiv/NSAEBB/NSAEBB82/

Kate Moss snorting cocaine

gawker.com

http://www.gawker.com/news/drugs/kate-moss-in-cocaine-nonshocker-contd-125768.php

ISBN 1-4013-0290-4

Hyperion books are available for special promotions and premiums.
For details contact Michael Rentas, Assistant Director, Inventory Operations,
Hyperion, 77 West 66th Street, 12th floor, New York, New York 10023, or
call 212-456-0133.

FIRST EDITION

10   9   8   7   6   5   4   3   2   1